Take Relief

Uncover the
Myths & Misunderstandings
of Golf Performance

By Sam Jarman

A catalogue record for this book is available from the British Library

Print ISBN: 978-0-9935734-3-9

Cover image by Mark Herreid, distributed by Shutterstock.com

Table of Contents

Acknowledgements   v

Foreword   vii

Chapter 1: Introduction   1

Chapter 2: Why Are You Reading This Book?   15

Chapter 3: Is Golf Psychology Working?   29

Chapter 4: Myth 1—Enjoyment Depends On
How You Play   47

Chapter 5: Myth 2—Good Golf Is Consistent Golf   69

Chapter 6: Myth 3—State of Mind Matters   89

Chapter 7: Myth 4—Control the Controllables   109

Chapter 8: Myth 5—Hard Work Ensures Success   129

Chapter 9: Myth 6—Learning Golf Is Difficult   145

Chapter 10: Conclusion   163

Author's note   183

About the Author   185

Acknowledgements

This book was a different experience from writing *The Three Principles of Outstanding Golf*. It seemed less of a struggle. I didn't set out to write the previous book. It started as an article for my website and just kept going.

This time was different. I knew there were things in *Three Principles* that needed clarification, and my understanding moved on almost the moment the book was published. In that regard *Take Relief* is the next step on the journey.

There are many people I would like to thank for their help and support along the way.

My dear friend Garret Kramer, whose words set me on this path nearly 10 years ago. His clarity and depth of understanding continue to be a source of inspiration and guidance.

Adam Ashe, Grayson Hart and Rich Hudson who happily have become colleagues as well as close friends. Likewise, Dr Lee Adair-Stantiall for her advice and clarification in the chapter on psychology and suggestions for other sections of the book.

Editor Joel Drazner for his patience, attention to detail and incisive questioning on the numerous occasions when the point I thought I was making was less than clear.

Julia Jarman, who remains a far better writer than I will ever be. Her love of books and the written word was a constant theme throughout my childhood and was clearly more of an inspiration than I realised at the time.

Phil Hughes, Ken Smith, Ken Minter, Alex Collman, Eddie Martin, Dan Hanlon and numerous others who offered comments, feedback and encouragement during the writing process.

David Cowap for his help and advice with the cover design and typesetting.

Lastly, my friends, lesson clients and fellow golfers at Woburn and elsewhere, for your friendship, feedback, support and companionship on and off the golf course.

Hopefully the ongoing conversation has made golf a more enjoyable experience for us all and will continue to do so.

Foreword

I met Sam in November 2015 in London at a talk. We didn't know it at the time, but that day was the start of a close friendship and an ongoing conversation, about the nature of high performance and mental wellbeing in sport and life.

As a professional rugby player, I'm often pointed to what other people believe the source of excellence and consistency to be. Mostly outwards towards 'how tos' and behaviours, visible symptoms, effects.

In the modern sporting world we are conditioned to latch on to things that are tangible and measurable.

Some coaches point to a player's stats. Others believe that a great environment or culture is the key. Some players believe that performance is enhanced by finding a nice partner and being settled off the pitch.

Many fans believe that a player's motivation comes from being successful or earning a lot of money. Psychologists or performance coaches will suggest that focus and peace of mind can be attained by applying a technique or practising a mantra.

At some point, everyone has experienced well-being, excellence and contentment. Somewhere within us we have an inkling that it wasn't caused directly by the past or the future, by what we acquired, achieved or what has happened to us.

In sports and in a society where psychological struggle is on the rise, we rarely consider whether our true nature could be the source of our happiness. Yet when we look past our conditioned beliefs and explore our direct experience, we see that it can't be found anywhere else.

It's our birthright. A knowing that occasionally gets clouded due to a set of beliefs that we take to be true. It's the one thing we share that lies at the very source of the mind.

Our attention is constantly focused on objects; thoughts, ideas, the future, the past, people and circumstances. All of this arises within something. What is the space in between two thoughts? We take it to be nothing important, because it doesn't have much to say. It's silent. But the words on this page cannot exist without the white space that surrounds them?

Our minds love to point to things in the world

to justify why we feel the way we do.

"It's because of what I was thinking."

"It's because the weather was great today."

"It's because we had a good weeks training."

What if the freedom we felt was actually the attachment to these things falling away? The knowing that shines in our heart that we are way more than what we may be thinking in any moment. Could this recognition help us deliver consistency of performance regardless of the objects and perceptions that show up in our experience?

You could call it a deeper recognition of being OK, even when thoughts may suggest otherwise.

As young athletes, at a certain age a question comes to mind. "What do I need to do to reach my potential? How can I perform as consistently as I possibly can?"

This question and the search which follows normally takes us away from the source. We look to techniques, visualisations and practices. They can be helpful for people to a degree. They can also be detrimental.

If a player begins to believe that the source of confidence or great performance comes from the thing they did, that belief will take the player further into the world of form, and further from the true source of excellence, happiness and contentment.

I was on that path after being introduced to visualisation techniques and mantras. Slowly over time I became confused as the techniques stopped working. My exclusive focus on them made me feel more anxious rather than when I allowed the mind to relax. Without knowing I began to cloud the innate potential and wisdom which had been guiding me. I stopped feeling the freedom I experienced when playing as a boy.

Confidence, consistency and contentment drifted away.

In the blink of an eye, we can fall of out misunderstanding. We can be reminded by our heart, which is what guided us to play as young kids. This fortunately happened for me. We can enjoy our sport with more ease and clarity. We begin living full out, we let go of misunderstandings and concepts, throwing ourselves into the game knowing that our wellbeing never goes anywhere.

The following pages will clear up many of the misunderstandings and myths which plague the mental side of sport.

The knowing that Sam points the reader towards is universal. The understanding in this book will benefit everyone, not just golfers, and not just on the field of play.

Adam Ashe
Professional Rugby Player
Glasgow Warriors and Scotland

"It is the real secret of life – to be completely engaged with what you are doing in the here and now. And instead of calling it work, realise it is play."

Alan Watts

CHAPTER 1

Introduction

I PLAYED HIGH-LEVEL GOLF for 10 years, starting in the early 1990s as an elite amateur, and then as a professional. I have been a coach since 2007.

Over the past 20 years, I have seen many theories, concepts and strategies aimed at helping golfers become more consistent, play their best golf in important tournaments, and enjoy the game as much as they remember doing when they started playing.

Unfortunately, these techniques and approaches seem to have the opposite effect than intended. They all have the same damaging flaw. They encourage golfers to think about what they are doing and how they are doing it.

I have asked many of the golfers I have coached and played with over the past 20 years the same question:

"What are you thinking about when you play

your best?"

I usually get one of two answers.

"Nothing," or "I have no idea."

When golfers are struggling, they invariably have a lot of thinking. Suffering from information overload, they get in their own way. Swing thoughts. Strategy and decisions. Things to do. Things not to do. What ifs. If onlys.

This leads us to the first—and perhaps most-important—question this book will address:

Can a human being control or divert the flow of thought?

If you've ever tried to manage or manipulate the content of your felt or perceived experience, you might have wondered about this. Most golfers have at some point attempted to block out the thought of missing a putt, to change an uncomfortable feeling or to have a more positive mindset.

It is implied that most golf psychology or performance-coaching approaches will help us to manage our thoughts and feelings and to control our state of mind. But do these interventions make golfers play better? Do golfers enjoy playing more now than they did when they first took up the game?

Look to your current experience, how you feel

about your game right now. Would you be reading this book if you didn't think that playing better might make you happier?

In the following pages, I will ask some questions that will point in a different direction to that suggested in most golf instruction books, magazines and videos. There will be no positive thinking, no visualising, no routines and no 'five step plans' to boost motivation or build confidence.

We will examine some of the common misunderstandings about the 'inner game' that have taken root in our golfing culture, and in sport generally, over the past few decades.

I hope this book will simplify your approach to playing your best golf. It will clarify what is important in terms of performance and enjoyment, and expose what is myth, superstition and self-deception.

Six Myths About 'The Inner Game'

Here are six common beliefs about the mental side of golf. How many of these do you think are true?

1. Your feelings when you play are affected directly by external factors. The significance of the competition, your previous performances, who you are playing with, and the difficulty of the golf course can all

have an impact. Confidence results from playing well, and it can be damaged by a bad shot or a bad round.

2. The key to golfing success and enjoyment is consistency. This leads to other beliefs. For example, that in order to play your best golf more often, you need to follow a consistent pre-shot routine, to practice hitting the same shot over and over again, to visualise good shots, and to have a repeatable golf swing.

3. You need to be in a confident, calm, relaxed, focused or other positive state of mind to play well. Golfers spend time and energy monitoring and then trying to either maintain or change how they feel in the belief that one mindset is better than another and will lead to improved play.

4. You need to 'control the controllables'. The best golfers always think positive, overcome doubts, feel motivated and are the masters of their golf swings, ball flight and emotions.

5. Hard work is the key to success. You need to perfect your swing technique and groove your putting stroke. You need to become mentally tough. When these things are done, you will play well all the time.

6. In order to learn and develop, you need to figure out and be in conscious control of the

learning process. You need to have a 'growth mindset'. Golf will be more enjoyable when you are a better player than you are now.

How many of the six beliefs do you subscribe to? I know my behaviour during my playing career was shaped by all of them. In the following pages, we will question these concepts. We will try to find out why, if they are true, so many golfers who abide by them are struggling.

What if these ideas are taking us further from what we are looking for, rather than bringing it closer?

Better Information, Faster Learning

This book seemed easier to write than my previous one. Perhaps because exposing what isn't true is easier than trying to describe what is. Inspiration arose whenever I went to my bookshelf, picked up one of a dozen or so golf-psychology books, blew the dust off and started reading. A few pages in, I'd get annoyed and frustrated at the strategies suggested, and the ideas and words would flow.

So many myths and misunderstandings have sprung up over the years and then been repeated by well-meaning coaches, sports psychologists and commentators. Theory becomes accepted as fact.

I'm sure these books were written with the best of intentions. As an author all you can do is share your perspective from a moment in time. That these ideas became accepted laws about how golfers think and feel just shows the strength of an illusion most of us never escape from.

That our wellbeing and happiness depend on the circumstances of our lives.

This illusion gives rise to the beliefs we will examine in the rest of the book. Doing so will perhaps allow you to trust your own gut instinct and common sense more than you do at present. To follow your heart as much as your head.

The aim is to simplify rather than complicate. To strip away layers of thinking rather than add. To reveal truth rather than obscure it.

Unfortunately, the swing-technique side and the mental side of the game of golf have gone in opposite directions. One has become more definitive, the other has become more confused.

Our understanding of what happens when a golf club strikes a golf ball has become clearer. Launch monitors, motion sensors and high-speed cameras have made it possible to get better-quality information than ever before about how the golfer's body, the club and the ball interact during a swing or stroke.

We no longer need to estimate or guess. The days of a coach suggesting to a player that her swing might have 'come over the top a bit', or that she 'got ahead of that one' are hopefully coming to an end.

We can clearly see the combination of face angle, club path, speed and angle of attack that caused the ball to fly or roll in the way it did. For many good instructors, this has meant a simplification of how they now teach the game.

The first step is to help students fully understand the principles and implications of the ball flight laws. The second is to help them to feel what their own swing is really doing. Is it delivering the clubface to the ball in a manner that, according to those laws, will produce the desired ball flight?

With good understanding and awareness of the swing, golfers will often find their own 'best way' of creating a functional blend of club face alignment, path, speed and angle of attack with minimal 'how to' input from the coach.

When golfers have a clear understanding of the task, they have a much better chance of completing it successfully. Young players these days, in terms of their understanding of what makes a golf swing powerful and efficient, are miles ahead of where I was at the same age.

Access to accurate information speeds up the learning process by exposing blind alleys and eliminating wild goose chases.

Unfortunately, the field of sports psychology seems to be heading in the opposite direction to that of golf-swing coaching.

Strategies and techniques are put forward, often based on the latest interpretation of brain science or learning theory. Rather than simplifying and clarifying our understanding of the human experience, further layers of complexity are added. They lead to more theories about what golfers need to think, or must not think, in order to play well. Many of these strategies collapse under a simple examination of cause and effect.

Reading the Mental Map

We all have a set of mental constructs, a mind map, of how we believe the world to be. Within this map, are theories about relative aspects of how that world works. We struggle when our beliefs about how golf should be and the reality of it fail to match up. In other words, when the map turns out to be inaccurate.

Unfortunately, our faith in the map is very strong. We become very attached to the ideas of how reality should look so that we might feel happy. When a conflict between belief and experience happens and our mood darkens, we blame the world for being out of sympathy with how we think it should be, rather than entertaining the possibility it might be the other way around.

'Reality' is how it is *regardless of our ideas or beliefs about it.* Unfortunately, most people prefer their beliefs over their own direct experience. As you can imagine, this leads to a good deal of anxiety and distress. Trying to change the world to match your expectations is a frustrating and time-consuming endeavour.

Imagine you had a tourist map of London. As you travel around, you discover that some of the landmarks depicted on the map don't match what you see when you arrive at the location. This is frustrating, but the map was free, so you make notes of the errors and keep going about your business. You adjust your map to suit what you discover to be true.

What you don't do is start making plans to have roads and buildings moved to match the piece of paper you were given.

Based on our actual experiences, we constantly make small adjustments to our mental maps of how the world really is. It's a built-in function of the human operating system. We call it learning.

When things go wrong, one of two things has happened:

We've forgotten that the map is just an interpretation of reality, and we try to change the outside world to match our beliefs. Or we've forgotten that map adjustments happen naturally, and we try to manually override or force the learning process.

Both courses of action lead to annoyance, frustration and thoughts that we are helpless, incompetent, or both.

A Plan of Action

Initially, we will look at how our mental maps of the world of golf are currently drawn. We will explore the relationship between our thoughts and feelings.

We will examine how thought works. How the beliefs and ideas that make up our mental map come to be and are updated and adjusted. You will see how a better understanding of thought is a game changer when it comes to getting out of your own way.

With a better understanding of the system, you might see that letting it work as intended, rather than fighting it, gives you a better chance of playing the golf you are capable of more often.

The most important moment in my adult life was the moment I saw that reality wasn't what I believed it to be. My map was fundamentally flawed. The world worked differently to the way I had come to believe.

I don't know exactly when confusion set in. But I seem to remember that up to age 11 or 12, life seemed simple and straightforward, becoming increasingly more difficult and complicated from then on. So, I guess that was the time when I started to get more caught up in the powerful illusion mentioned earlier.

I'm sure it didn't happen overnight, but I slipped into a belief that my wellbeing was conditional on what happened to me, on my outside circumstances. On how well I was doing at school, on the sports field and in my relationships.

Once this belief took hold, it seemed the only option was to keep monitoring, judging and manipulating those circumstances so I would feel happy more often than not.

I struggled and strived, thought more, worried more, worked harder. Sometimes I was successful. But even when things were going well, I became insecure about losing what I had. Low-level frustration, anxiety and self-doubt persisted throughout my teens and early adulthood, both on and off the golf course.

I was in my late 30s when I was shown the nature of the misunderstanding I had been living under. Golf and life looked simple again. I felt the freedom to just play as I had done when I was a young boy.

For our behaviour to change, for us to drop old habits, we usually need to let go of something we believe to be true, but isn't. This is why so many of us get stuck. We prefer to cling to our beliefs rather than opening our eyes, our hearts and our minds to the light of our direct experience. To the present moment.

I hope this book will assist you in so doing. That you might feel able to question what you currently believe to be true about your golf. Does every thought you have about the game need to be taken seriously? To what extent are you in control of what you think and, as a result, of how you feel?

Why does it seem that you need to become something more, someone better, in order to enjoy your golf again?

If you can find the courage to question those long-standing and strongly held beliefs, a range of new possibilities for you and your golf might arise.

A belief or mindset is just a thought that we

take more seriously than other thoughts. It is usually propped up and supported by a framework of habitual thinking and confirmation bias, built up over time.

Fortunately, it only takes one insight for a strongly held belief to be relegated back down to the level of 'just another thought'.

I'm sure you can think of beliefs that you didn't question some years ago, which don't make much sense today. Father Christmas? The tooth fairy? That the sun rises and falls?

With these examples in mind, let's set a challenge for the rest of the book.

What are you going to trust more—your existing belief structure, or your direct experience in this, the present moment?

One will keep you stuck where you are. The other can set you free.

CHAPTER 2

Why Are You Reading This Book?

WHEN I'M NOT PLAYING GOLF, writing or coaching, my favourite distraction is fishing. More precisely, salmon fishing. The Atlantic salmon is one of the most prized sporting fish in the world. It is powerful, elusive and is found in some of the wildest and most beautiful places on earth.

Sadly, due to years of overfishing and river mismanagement, catching an Atlantic salmon is increasingly difficult.

Many anglers go for weeks at a time without hooking a fish. So, when the line eventually does tighten, the moment lives long in the memory.

Living the Dream

A keen angler had been looking forward to his fishing holiday for many months.

He spent the preceding weeks watching the weather forecast and preparing his tackle. He packed a wide range of lines and lures to ensure he could cope with whatever challenge the river conditions might present.

The long drive north was filled with anticipation. He arrived at his rented cottage in the late afternoon. After a good meal and a couple of pints at the local pub, he was in bed before closing time, ready for an early start.

The following morning, conditions were perfect as he arrived at the fishing hut on the bank of the river. The water was at an ideal height and temperature. The ghillie (his fishing guide) said that a large run of salmon had come in from the sea on the recent high tides. The anticipation increased as he pulled on his waders and set up the rod and line.

Hands shaking as he tied a favourite fly onto the end of the line, his heart skipped a beat as a big silver fish leapt out of the pool in front of him before crashing back into the peaty water.

With a dry mouth and a racing pulse, he walked upstream through the pine forest to the head of the pool. He carefully waded across the shallows, pulled a few yards of line from the reel and began to cast, gradually increasing the distance until he was covering the water close to the far bank.

The lure swung across the river in a shallow arc

as the line was carried downstream by the current. As it came over the main flow into the quieter water on the near side, there was a large boil on the surface of the water, then a determined tug, tug, tug on the line.

A fish had taken the fly!

Any salmon fisherman will tell you that the take is the most exciting, most magical part of the whole experience. The feeling is indescribable. Addictive, like hitting a drive right out the middle of the club, or rolling a long putt, dead weight into the centre of the hole.

The fly was hooked securely in its top jaw. After a good fight the fish was ready to be landed. The angler carefully weighed it, took a photograph, then gently supported it in the current until it had recovered sufficiently to swim away.

He was ecstatic. A fresh run 20-pounder on the first run down the pool! The stuff dreams are made of!

When his pulse had returned to normal, he walked quietly back up to the head of the pool. Taking a couple of paces downstream in between each cast, he carefully fished down to the same spot. The fly plopped into the quiet water by the far bank. Swinging slowly over the main part of the current, again there was a strong draw on the line.

Another fish! This was incredible! To catch one the first morning of his holiday was a pleasant surprise. Two was unbelievable!

Again, it was well hooked. After a few heart-stopping moments as it ran downstream through the rapids into the pool below, it was safely landed by the ghillie before being released back into the river.

He walked up to the head of the pool for a third time and proceeded to cast across, gradually lengthening line until he was covering the full width of the river. He reached the same spot, when, for a third time in the space of a few minutes, the line went tight, and a large salmon leapt from the water. Shaking its head, the fish charged off across the river taking yards of line with it.

The fisherman was stunned. Nothing like this had ever happened to him before.

Barely believing what was happening, he care-fully played the fish to the net again before weighing it, taking a picture and releasing it back into the stream. He was in heaven. It just didn't get any better than this.

Three fresh-run salmon in one morning! Thank

goodness he had pictures and the ghillie as a witness. No one would believe him otherwise! Thoughts of interviews with fishing magazines and articles in the local paper raced across his mind.

After a short break to settle down, he walked downstream through the heather and silver birch trees to another of his favourite pools.

Again, he made a few casts across the river. Again, as he reached the middle of the pool a salmon took the fly. Astonishing! That run of fish must be huge. He played it to the net and released it back to continue its journey upstream.

Five minutes later from the same place, exactly the same result!

And again.

And again.

With every fourth or fifth cast producing a similar large fish, even the excitement of the take dwindled. He was almost expecting it. He suddenly noticed his arms were sore, and his back ached. Gradually his enthusiasm for playing yet another salmon dropped away.

He sat down on the river bank. His head was spinning as he slowly came to the awful realisation. It wasn't a dream he was having.

It was a nightmare.

The Balance Between Challenge and Mastery

Most golfers will understand the paradox in this story and the parallels with golf.

The game is a physical and mental challenge. It's hard to play it well. No matter how good you become, there are always dreams that you could improve, and nagging thoughts that form could desert you at any moment. Trying to realise the former can lead to the latter. If golf was easy, would we be as captivated as so many of us are?

Once you solve a Rubik's Cube, you don't want to play with it every day. A joke isn't as funny when you know the punchline. A thriller isn't thrilling when you know the ending.

For the recreational golfer, it's hard to imagine that shooting in the 60s every time you step onto a golf course could become tiresome. Yet, over the years, many successful golfers have lost their enthusiasm for the game. Some start looking for other challenges or distractions to get the buzz they once got from golf, occasionally with unfortunate consequences.

It seems that seeking is human nature. Even when successful, we want more. We look for the next challenge, to prove ourselves once again.

When our feelings for golf change over time, as they inevitably will, it's important to realise that the game itself hasn't.

The game of golf is neutral. How we feel about it depends on our expectations, our beliefs and the judgements we make. It depends on who or what we believe ourselves to be in that moment.

Which brings us to an important question . . .

What Sort of Golfer Are You?

Let's get it out of the way early so we know where we're at. Cards on the table, so to speak.

I doubt you would be reading this book if you were playing to your potential and loving your golf. Or if you didn't think that improving might make you happier than you are now.

You would be out on the course or the driving range enjoying yourself. Or getting some other stuff done so that you can go and play or practice later.

Every golfer has their own reasons for playing. How well do you understand yourself? What makes you pick up the clubs and head out for a few holes? What do you want from the game? Would knowing make the experience more enjoyable? I hope this book might help you answer these questions, and to see more clearly what golf means to you.

If you stop enjoying the game, it's probably because your standard of play isn't meeting your expectations. But is your game poor, or are your expectations unrealistic? Where is the sweet spot between your ability and the challenge? The first step to getting back on track is often to figure out exactly what is going on. Where are those feelings of lack coming from?

Below, I have described four types of golfer.

They are caricatures, but hopefully they will give you an idea of where you might currently be on the spectrum of golfing satisfaction. They might help to pinpoint the reason you picked up this book.

1. You aren't playing well, and as a result you aren't enjoying the game.

> This is a common situation. Golf feels like hard work. You think you need to improve some parts of your game in order to play better. You believe that when you play better you will enjoy the game again.
>
> You have tried lessons, magazines, YouTube videos—the usual routes to improving—but the results haven't been what

you had hoped. You are looking for some fresh ideas before you find a new teacher and buy another new driver.

2. Golf is fun most of the time, but you want to improve and play better more often.

You're a bit frustrated. The improvement in your game seems to have plateaued. You have had the same handicap for a while, and you seem to keep coming up against different variations of the same obstacles. You can't get all the parts of your game working well at the same time.

You are passionate about golf and suspect that those feelings come partly from the challenge of it. You just wish you had a clearer picture of what you need to do to reach the goals you have set.

3. You are playing OK, but you just aren't enjoying your golf as much as you used to.

The enthusiasm you used to feel for the game isn't there. You aren't excited about playing or practising any more. You aren't getting out as much as you used to and are worried you might have had enough of it. What will you do with yourself if you don't play golf?

You wonder if a different approach will help you enjoy the game again, but you don't know what it is or where to look for it.

4. You could be in all three of those categories. How you play and how you feel about your golf varies from day to day.

> You have good days and bad days. You're aware that golf is like that. You'd like to get a better understanding of how your mind works. About why you feel how you feel about your golf from day to day and week to week.

> (You secretly hope that understanding yourself better might knock a few shots off your handicap and win you a few club competitions.)

What Do You Want From the Game?

Likely you can identify with one or more of those categories. It might surprise you that the remedy for all these apparently different issues can be found in the same simple understanding.

For most people, it looks like several different things need to happen for them to enjoy the game. I'll list them shortly. The following chapters are intended help you to clarify the relationship between events and your feelings. In doing so, your investment in the game might make more sense.

You may think you already know what would make that investment seem worthwhile. If so, that's great.

Just hang in there, though, because a lot of people think they know. But when the question is asked another way, they find the answer changes.

OK, that list I mentioned. Most people would like:

To play to their expectations more often.

To get their handicap down.

To improve their golf swing.

To win a few competitions or beat their friends.

To enjoy the game they invest so much time, effort and money in.

None of which will probably come as a surprise. But it's the next question that causes the head scratching.

Why do you want those things?

What would achieving or accomplishing them do for you? Would the way you feel about your golf, or about yourself change? Take a moment to have a think and maybe jot down a few ideas. At the end of the book, it might be interesting to see if those answers would be different.

I'm aware that some golfers have no interest in exploring the more cerebral aspects of their chosen pastime. They play well, they enjoy it. They play badly, they don't. Either way, it isn't a problem.

If that's you, let's not set off a train of unnecessary and irrelevant thinking. Please put the book down and head to the driving range or onto the golf course. It's all good. No hard feelings. (Just come back to it if you change your mind.)

If, on the other hand, you are interested in knowing a bit more about why the game grips you as it does, and how you might play it a bit better, please read on.

In the coming chapters, I'm going to point towards the real reasons why golfers find it so hard to improve. Why they enjoy the game one day but not the next. Why they struggle to play their best golf when they really want to.

I doubt you will have heard these ideas anywhere else, although the understanding that underpins them has been around for thousands of years.

I believe we are at the beginning of a new era in understanding where golfing performance comes from. And the good news is, our love for the game originates from the same place. Nowhere in the rules of golf does it say that you must struggle and grind in order to play well. Great golf and enjoyment can co-exist.

But to experience them more often, we might need to kill a few sacred cows. These take the form of ideas and beliefs that almost certainly affect how you feel and the decisions you make whenever you step out onto the golf course.

These theories are so deeply ingrained in golfing culture, it's unlikely that you have questioned whether they might not be true.

Let the myth busting begin!

CHAPTER 3

Is Golf Psychology Working?

I'M NOT A PSYCHOLOGIST.

I jumped at the chance to study it at A-Level, but quickly became disillusioned. I couldn't see how the statistical element (which seems to be a major part of the subject) was relevant in helping people understand their thoughts and feelings.

To be honest, I still don't.

Some of the theories about how the brain works are interesting. But I don't see how it's possible to change someone else's thoughts or fix their un-wanted behaviour. Most therapies, interventions, techniques, strategies, or methods work with the same level of consistency as an 18 handicappers golf swing.

I occasionally get challenged by a psychologist who believes that in order to help people who are struggling with their feelings to find relief, you need to have had years of training from other psychologists.

I'm not sure what qualifications are required to offer someone support, kindness and to encourage a different type of enquiry into the nature of their current experience.

If you come from a paradigm that sees a suffering person as 'broken', that it's your job to fix them, then I guess that having a toolbox of approaches and therapies to use might make sense.

If you live in a paradigm where you believe that someone is feeling the way they feel because of the situation or circumstances of their lives, then offering strategies to help them cope with those circumstances, or to suggest ways to change them, might seem like a good idea.

The warnings from psychologists that 'patients' could be damaged by an intervention from an unqualified person might be an unintended judgement on the methods that are practised in that profession. Electric-shock therapy is still administered to depressed individuals in the hope of curing them.

If you appreciate that we all struggle from time to time when we lose sight of the true nature of our experience, then you start from the point of view that no one is broken. With that understanding, to suggest that a bagful of approaches, techniques and therapies are needed to help someone, looks like a case of the blind leading the blind.

Why not just offer love and support and point to the misunderstanding that is the source of the suffering?

Might that not be a kinder, gentler and ultimately more productive way of helping than insisting the sufferer relives past traumatic events and 'deals with them'?

Contradiction and Confusion

For the past 150 years, the study of human psychology has been confusing and confused. The field has been spread wide with numerous theories, hypotheses, ideas and speculations.

Many of these theories are contradictory. They are based on correlations that are observed and judged to be significant, rather than on scientific method, which can be rigorously tested.

Sports psychology is no different. Many techniques and approaches offered to golfers are based on observations and subjective interpretations that don't stand up under the scrutiny of either common sense or our direct experience. I know this. I spent most of my playing career trying to make them work despite the doubts I had at the time.

Looking back, I can see that when I played well, it was despite whatever mental strategies I was employing at the time, rather than because of them.

If you're a sports psychologist reading this book, I acknowledge that describing as myths and superstitions the interventions you are offering to your clients might be troubling. You have probably invested a considerable amount of time and money on an education that you now worry might be wasted.

There is another way of looking at it.

A number of my colleagues come from different branches of the field of psychology. It would be understandable if they felt insecure about, or even threatened by, a new and different understanding of the nature of human experience that says pretty much the opposite to what they learned at university.

Instead, they have embraced this new perspective and quietly incorporated it into their work, often with impressive results.

Dr George Pransky was a clinical psychologist for 20 years before he had an insight into the true nature of how the mind works. Upon the realisation that feelings are generated moment to moment via thought, rather than caused directly by our situation or circumstances, he said:

"I saw that I had just spent the past 25 years learning about the history of psychology. I had extensive experience of what helped people and what didn't. With my new understanding, I now saw why certain approaches worked while others didn't. And more important, I knew the underlying reasons for both success and failure."

It's my hope that more people currently working in the field of sports psychology will start to look beyond the attachment they have to strategies and mind-management techniques.

Deep down, many of these well-meaning individuals realise through their own direct experience that these interventions don't work consistently and therefore fail to serve the people that they are trying to help.

What Is Psychology?

There are several definitions, the most common being 'the study of the human mind and behaviour.' Most people understand and can describe behaviour. But what do we really mean by 'the human mind'?

Is it the brain? Is it something more nebulous, less tangible?

Thinking? Feeling? Perceiving? Is it an object, or

an activity?

The lack of a clear definition and blurred parameters of what is being studied might explain why the field of sports psychology finds itself in such a confused and fragmented state.

It doesn't really know what it is. Or what its function is. Coaches and players are confused by the terminology and methodology of the research. Researchers don't know how to transfer their findings from an academic environment to the field of play.

Is it sports science? A social science? Is it a field of academia? Is it a branch of philosophy, biology or sports medicine?

As it stands, it seems wrong to describe psychology as a science. Unlike the hard sciences, physics and chemistry, there isn't an established set of principles, or laws against which theories and hypotheses can be evaluated and tested.

Much of what psychology is attempting to study can't be measured or quantified. How does one judge the relative importance of a thought? Or objectively measure the strength of a feeling such as confidence or composure? In trying to quantify such things we are completely reliant on the perception of the experience by the person describing it.

It is subjective.

Can you accurately remember how confident, relaxed or nervous you were the last time you played golf? Did the feeling last for the whole round or did it ebb and flow? If you can't recall accurately, how can you compare it to another occasion when you might have felt something similar? Or something different?

Human perception is not an accurate representation of reality. Memory of those perceptions is even less reliable.

Many psychological studies are conducted by asking questions about how someone is or was feeling. Setting aside the likelihood that asking such questions could lead to a change in the way someone feels, these so-called 'qualitative surveys' are inevitably subjective.

If an academic endeavour cannot define itself, or agree on how it measures whatever it is supposed to be measuring, how can it know what is being studied or how to draw conclusions from what is observed?

This problem was identified as far back as 1890 by American philosopher William James, widely regarded as the founder of modern psychology.

He stated that until the principles of psychology were established, the field would remain confused and fragmented. While James predicted that principles would one day be uncovered and defined, confusion remains to this day.

For psychology to be able to defend itself against suggestions of being a pseudoscience, the field needs to agree upon a set of fundamental truths. Agreeing a set of principles or laws would underpin research, allow theories to be tested, further discussion and lead to a deeper understanding.

What Is a Principle?

In the absence of such agreement, the following pages suggest a framework that might help golfers better understand their thoughts and feelings. The first step is to establish a definition for a principle. When we recognise a principle, we can understand the implications of that principle in the light of our experience. We will explore this in more depth shortly.

The *Oxford English Dictionary* offers the following definitions of *principle*:

> "A fundamental, primary or general law, from which others are derived. For example, the principles of modern physics."

Or:

"A fundamental truth or proposition that serves as the foundation for a system of belief or behaviour, or for a chain of reasoning."

And:

A fundamental source or basis of something. 'The first principle of all things was water.'

What properties or attributes would a principle have in the context of understanding more about the relationship between our thoughts and feelings?

The following criteria have been suggested by clinical psychologist Dr Keith Blevens. Dr Blevens is a pioneer of what is sometimes known as the 'Inside-Out understanding'—that our feelings are a result of thought, not circumstance.

A principle is:

1. **Constant.** *A principle is always true. It never varies. There are no exceptions.*
2. **Explanatory.** *A principle provides a complete account for how something works. There are no anomalies.*
3. **Predictive.** *Given the principle, one can predict outcomes in advance.*

As an example of how such definitions might be helpful in the real world, we can test these attributes in the context of hitting a golf shot using a well-known principle of physics.

Newton's first law of motion states that 'an object at rest will remain at rest, and an object in motion remains in motion until acted on by another object or force.'

This scientific principle allows us to determine:

that given identical impact factors, launch conditions and atmospheric conditions a golf ball will have the same flight, trajectory and landing point every single time it is struck *(the principle is a constant).*

that the forces acting on the ball at impact were what caused it to fly in the manner it did *(the principle is explanatory).*

how changes in the forces applied to the golf ball at impact would cause the ball flight to be different *(the principle is predictive).*

For example, if the club head is moving faster at impact, all other factors being equal, the ball will travel further.

An *implication* is something that can be explained by, or is in relation to, a *principle.*

For example, a putt that rolls to the edge of the hole but doesn't fall in can also be explained by Newton's first law of motion as stated above.

The *implication* is that gravity and friction—the forces acting to slow the rolling ball—were strong enough to overcome the energy imparted at impact by the swinging club head before the ball reached the point where gravity could pull it to the bottom of the cup.

The principles of the 'hard' sciences—physics and chemistry—have been well established for many years. Some have been updated or superseded as our understanding of the world has deepened.

Understanding the implications of principles uncovered by Newton, Einstein, Faraday, Heisenberg, Dirac and Bohm, has enabled the building of bridges and skyscrapers, communication over vast distances, travel across oceans and continents and the investigation of other planets. The entirety of human knowledge can be summoned to a battery powered device that can be carried in a pocket.

Uncovering principles has changed the course of human history.

Unfortunately, the field of psychology lags in relation to these other fields of science. We could describe it as being in a *'pre-principles paradigm'*.

Before Ignatz Semmelweis's theory of germs and bacteria was accepted, the field of medicine languished in a similar situation. Lavoisier's development of the periodic table altered the paradigm in which chemistry was studied.

Change is coming. Principles of psychology are being uncovered. I believe they will become widely recognised and accepted in the coming months and years.

In the past, it has taken decades, sometimes centuries, for new paradigms to become mainstream. The speed by which information and ideas can be developed, challenged and shared via the internet will mean that new perspectives will take far less time to become the norm.

Once Semmelweis uncovered how germs and bacteria caused illness and death, educating doctors, nurses and medical professionals to wash their hands and sterilise their instruments improved the physical health of millions of people.

Establishing principles for psychology will have a similar impact on mental health.

Mind, Consciousness and Thought

While no concept from the human intellect can be considered an absolute truth, the understanding described in my previous book has been a valuable step to realising more deeply how my experience is created.

The definition of these principles of human feeling and behaviour is simple, but profound. They were given the names 'Universal Mind', 'Universal Consciousness' and 'Universal Thought', by philosopher and author Sydney Banks, who had a revelatory psychological experience in 1973.

The sharing of his insight among his community in British Columbia, Canada, gave this understanding a toehold from where it has gradually become more widely acknowledged and shared around the world. Syd Banks's books and videos are available on several websites and sharing platforms.

The greatest steps forward in our development as a society, it seems, have come from simplifications in our understanding of how our experience of the world is created and realised.

Banks's concept is one of these simplifications. If the field of psychology moves in the direction he was pointing, I believe it will get back on track and become more relevant.

He describes these principles as follows in his book *The Missing Link*.

1. ***Thought.*** *"Thought is the creative agent we use to direct us through life. Thought is not reality, but it is through Thought that all realities are created."*

2. ***Consciousness.*** *"Consciousness is the gift of awareness. Consciousness allows the recognition of form, form being the expression of Thought."*

3. ***Mind.*** *"Every human mind has direct access to its experience here on earth, and the human mind always has access to its spiritual roots from whence it came."*

If one of these elements is missing, you would not have a human experience.

My interpretation of these principles has developed and changed somewhat since my last book was published. Through reading and listening to Syd Banks's early teachings, I saw more clearly the underlying nature of what he was pointing to.

As he himself explained on various occasions, these principles cannot be separated or exist in isolation. In that sense, they point to one principle rather than three. The eternal paradox is that the underlying truth to which they refer cannot be conceptualised or explained with intellectual ideas, words or concepts.

Banks referred to electricity as an analogy. It's

easier to see and feel what it does, than to see it and explain what it is.

Even wise sages and enlightened teachers find the true nature of the human experience hard to grasp and impossible to describe. But that makes them no different than anyone else. All that any of us can do is to examine more closely our current experience, to differentiate between what is true, and what is belief or conjecture.

Implications For Golf

The most powerful implication is often the simplest.

Once we can isolate and know for certain in what direction truth lies, we can also see definitively what ideas are not pointing in that direction. We can put aside a raft of myths and misunderstandings that might have been preventing us from playing to our potential and enjoying our golf.

By knowing for sure what is not true, numerous possibilities and distractions are swept away. We dramatically simplify the way we see things, both on and off the golf course. This clarity leads to better decisions and to actions that are appropriate. We can test the thought-feeling connection in our everyday lives, simply by being aware of how it works and asking some direct questions about what is happening.

You don't need a sophisticated research in-strument. You can use your own direct experience to cut through any doubts, rather than relying on beliefs, conditioning or someone else's thoughts, observations or concepts.

That's why it's important you don't take the words in this book at face value. They are a signpost, not a destination. I hope that you will be inspired to explore your own experience, to come to your own conclusions.

Just replacing one set of beliefs for another set doesn't move you closer to the truth.

Answers as to the true nature of the human mind will be found with a rigorous examination of deeply held theories, ideas and concepts. You will see clearly that much of what we take to be cause and effect, in golf and in life, is, in fact, correlation reinforced by confirmation bias. The intellect fabricates all sorts of theories and concepts to explain the way life seems to be unfolding.

From childhood, we are conditioned to follow the hypothesis that we are feeling a certain way because of 'something'. We then look outwards to the world of form to find what that 'something' might be. Our beliefs are always created in hind-sight.

We drive down the road looking in the rearview mirror.

In the next chapters, we will explore the conflict between belief and our direct experience. We will look at some of the myths that have built up around the way we play the game of golf. We will find out why they endure and what might be true about life and golf once we have seen beyond the misunderstanding.

What might that mean for us as golfers? As people? Could we play the games of golf and life in a simpler way than we currently believe is possible? We might come to realise that the struggles we face are innocently of our own making.

Rather than being something we need to work at, relief could be a single insight away as we gain a deeper understanding of our true nature.

CHAPTER 4

Myth 1—Enjoyment Depends On How You Play

IN CHAPTER 2, I ASKED: Why are you reading this book?

I feel I should apologise. It's a bit of a trick question. 'Why?' is a step on a path which ultimately leads back to where it came from. A mirage in a desert of intellectual knowledge. It hangs tantalisingly in front of you, but the answer is always just out of reach.

Notice how 'Why?' holds the promise of enlightenment but only ever leads to another 'Why?' It's like having a conversation with a curious child.

"Why A?" the child asks. "Because B," you reply.

"Why B?" asks the child. "Because C", you answer.

"Yes, but why C . . . ?"

There is no end to the apparent chain of causality in theoretical knowledge, because as any honest scientist will tell you, there are some things we just don't know yet.

What is the nature of consciousness? Where does thought come from?

If you ask the question 'Why do we play golf?' the obvious follow up is 'Why do we do anything? There is no ultimate answer to the question 'Why?' The logic behind that statement is the truth that underpins this understanding, to be further explored as we progress through the book.

Most golfers only think about why they play when they find it a struggle. I certainly don't remember ever questioning my motives when I was playing 45 holes a day during the long summer school holidays.

Golf was fun. I just played, practiced, learned and improved. I don't remember having any preconceptions about how I needed to hit the ball in order to enjoy myself. Or about what I was looking to get from the game when I stepped onto the first tee.

Knowing why you play is often put forward as the remedy for golf's psychological challenges. The argument being that if you know why you play, you will always be able to summon the right mindset and attitude with which to give your best effort. A clear purpose is a beacon of hope through the tough times, and it can help keep your feet on the ground in the good.

Or so the theory goes.

Back to the Future

If you are someone who has well-defined reasons for playing the game the way you play it, good for you. Nothing in this chapter is intended to muddy those clear waters.

Just play.

But if enjoyment is elusive, if you have lost your sense of purpose, it might be helpful to bear in mind that your reasons for playing are just your thoughts in the moment that you have them. Those thoughts are liable to change. They are no different in substance or value to a thought about what you might have for supper, or whether you should wear the blue shirt or the white one.

The same goes for your 'mindset'. A mindset is a belief. It is a thought or habit of thinking. It isn't where thinking, attitude or motivation originate. A mindset might appear more valuable than other thoughts because it supports or gives them credence. But this value is entirely self-certified by more thoughts.

I know from experience that golf is a lot less enjoyable if you question why you play every time you have a bad round. When I was younger, I seemed to get over things more quickly. A poor day was soon forgotten, rather than analysed.

I became curious about the game at 12 years old after watching Seve Ballesteros win the 1984 Open at St Andrews on television. It looked like a fun thing to do, so off I went into the garden. I vaguely remember constructing my first club from two bits of wood found in the garage.

Looking back, not having a clearly defined purpose other than having fun didn't detract from my enjoyment of the game.

In this regard, my golf has come full circle. For a large part of my professional career, I really didn't like the game (or myself) very much. There was a story about how golf needed to be in order for me to enjoy it. I thought I needed to play to a certain standard. If the reality didn't match up to the story, then it seemed I had a good reason to feel disappointed.

With the lack of enjoyment came the questions about why I was playing. I still felt relief and satisfaction when I did play well. I wanted more of those feelings so that looked like a reason to persevere. Another was the belief that all the time and effort I had put in over the years would be wasted unless I had something tangible to show for it: an end product; an outcome I could point to and say, "The struggle was worth it".

Looking back, these two 'reasons why I played' just stoked up the pressure I was putting on myself. I was playing tournaments for the results, because I felt I had to justify my previous investment, not because I enjoyed the experience. At the time, it looked like the feelings of dissatisfaction were coming directly from the game itself.

This, however, was never the case.

Happily, these days I'm back to having no other reason for playing the game than for its own sake. I enjoy the feeling of hitting the golf ball and watching it fly. When I stop enjoying it, I'll stop playing. The funny thing is, I'm playing as well now as I have ever done.

What Do You Want From Golf?

So, what do you think you need from the game in order to enjoy it? Lower scores? Longer drives? Respect from your friends and peers? Trophies? A single-figure handicap?

The question sits teasingly at the top of a long and slippery slope. Wanting any of these things isn't wrong. It's simply that once you want or need anything from anyone or anything outside you in order to be happy, you have fallen for the oldest illusion known to humanity.

It is the original sin.

We all know the feeling of neediness. It's an emotion we normally equate with relationships, money or status. It isn't a comfortable one.

Needy would be a good description of how I felt about my golf for a significant part of my playing career. Needy feelings, however, seem to be a strong repellent to the thing we sense that we lack. If you have read *The Three Principles of Outstanding Golf*, you might remember the 'I'll Be Happy When' game.

First described by my friend Jamie Smart, the game entails making your happiness conditional on an outside circumstance, something in the future. You work towards that goal, only to reach it and find that your happiness is short-lived. So, you set another goal and the search continues.

"I'll be happy when . . ."

As I found out, happiness and well-being have nothing to do with golf, or the situation or circumstances of your life. They are experienced when you stop making happiness and well-being conditional on golf and life. It is 100 percent an inside job.

I remember rounds of golf where I didn't play that well, but loved every minute. I've shot some low rounds where I have felt anxious and insecure the whole time, just waiting for the wheels to come off. My thought upon leaving the final green was, "Thank goodness that's over."

Realising where your feelings really come from is an important step on the path to fulfilling your potential as a golfer. Are you getting in your own way? Are you happy and at peace when you come off the golf course? Or are you disappointed, angry and frustrated, thinking about what might have been?

For most golfers, there will be a strong correlation between the score and how they feel. How did your golf measure up against your expectations? If you play better than the level you anticipated, then the post-round drink will be a happy one. If the performance is well below your expectations, the question will arise once more. "Why the hell do I play this stupid game?"

Uncomfortable feelings only come from thoughts about the past or the future. They are telling you to look to your current experience, to be in the present moment. If it seems like your game is making you unhappy, an honest appraisal of your expectations might be a good place to start. Anticipating the future, based on memories of the past is a pretty good way of getting in your own way.

As Tiger Woods is fond of saying, the game is what it is. Your feelings have nothing to do with how many times you hit the little white ball before it fell into the hole. The story you made up around what might happen and what it might mean was just that. A story.

If you feel anything other than happy and peaceful during or after the round, it's because you have identified with central character in the story about your golf and mistaken them for someone 'real'.

Just as an expectation is a thought, the person expecting is also a thought, or a collection of thoughts and feelings. As is the rest of the story—a thought, nothing more.

Thought—The Missing Link

Whether or not you have read *The Three Principles of Outstanding Golf*, it might be helpful to have a recap on the relationship between your circumstances and how you are feeling. As I mentioned previously, understanding this more clearly was a major milestone on the road to enjoying my golf again.

If you are asking yourself why you play, it's unlikely to be because you are tearing up the course and loving your golf.

The main reason people start questioning their motives for playing is because their enjoyment of the game is waning. It might well look like enjoyment is being denied because of the quality of your play, or the condition of the golf course, or the weather, or the people you are playing with.

When we feel there is no enjoyment, it is because we have had a thought that, in our opinion, things are not as they should be. It's a subjective judgement. It is a label we put on a situation where we feel a lack.

Our feelings are entirely independent of situation or circumstances. They depend on thought.

"Thought is the creative agent we use to direct us through life. Thought is not reality, but it is through Thought that all realities are created."

Sydney Banks

One of the ambitions for this book was that readers could evaluate any of the ideas using their own direct experience, rather than taking the words at face value. We don't need research to confirm *when* we are feeling happy or sad. Why does it seem so logical to seek help to understand the reasons *why*?

For example, if you ask yourself, "Am I aware that I think?" you shouldn't need help with the answer.

While a simple confirmation of an awareness of thought is a good place to start, some aspects of the nature of thinking aren't obvious. Looking at them more closely can help us understand more about ourselves both on and off the golf course.

Here are three things that become apparent when we become curious about the nature of our experience.

1. Our experience of the world is created via thought.

This might come as a bit of a shock, but the world we experience is not reality. In fact, it is continually created for us moment by moment via our thoughts and perceptions in real time.

From our subjective point of view, (which is itself a thought) our *experience* is 100 percent real.

But as we will explore in a later chapter, the true nature of what we think we are experiencing might be less tangible than most people realise.

Despite searching for hundreds of years, scientists have yet to come up with definitive proof that matter, the stuff the 'physical' world is made from actually exists in the way we think we experience it. Despite a lack of evidence, most of science takes the material world as a given and bases its assumptions on a relative comparison of phenomena in this 'physical' world.

So, if there is no evidence that a world made of matter exists, does it make sense to attribute our feelings to interactions with objects of that world?

Our felt experience is comprised of thoughts, perceptions and bodily sensations. We cannot feel, as many people believe they do, the situation or circumstances of our lives. The only feeling we can experience without thought isn't really a feeling in the same way that anger, or jealousy are feelings.

It's the true nature of our own being. We call this 'non-feeling' happiness, peace, or love.

Our experience of the world is created by thought, therefore we can feel differently from moment to moment about the same 'external' situation if our thinking about it changes. For the same reason, two people in the same circumstance can feel differently about it.

As thinking ebbs and flows, feelings will change independent of what is happening to us or around us.

2. *Thought is 'invisible' to most human beings, most of the time.*

Syd Banks referred to thought as 'the missing link.' Our experience is made entirely of our thoughts, feelings sensations and perceptions, but it's entirely normal that we forget we are thinking. We miss it. Our knowing of experience gets merged with experience, which means we forget our true nature. We forget who we really are.

We spend most of our lives unaware that thought is busy in the background creating an experience of a person experiencing a 'reality' from one moment to the next.

We think we are a body and mind experiencing 'the world', but in fact we are just experiencing thoughts, perceptions and sensations.

Thinking is invisible. The world looks 'real'. Therefore, the negative feelings that come along, and any troubling behaviours or habits that result from those feelings are entirely logical. If we saw thought for what it truly is, perhaps we would be less disturbed by our experience.

When we innocently forget the true nature of experience, we see the world as if it were real, and we feel and act in accordance with that misunderstanding. We will seek happiness in objects and achievements, and we will resist situations and circumstances that we believe might make us unhappy.

3. Thought is not a 'controllable'.

Personal thinking is a series of mentations; ideas, concepts, beliefs, images, memories and intuitions.

These appear randomly within awareness. Sometimes they seem highly inappropriate for the situation we are in. We can be frustrated, irritated or troubled at the content of our thinking. Most people have had the experience of walking into a room in their house and not being able to remember the reason they went there.

Would this occur if we could genuinely control what we thought and when we thought it? We are familiar with uncomfortable feelings when faced with a choice, or a decision. The illusion that we have agency leads us deeper into the mire.

The fact that we can have the thought, "I should know what the right answer is in this situation, but I don't", should point us to the fact that we don't have agency over what appears in awareness.

Thought is reliably unpredictable. Try to guess what you might be thinking about in an hour's time. Or to remember what you were thinking about an hour ago. We have no idea what will come into our awareness in the future, or when it will appear or disappear.

I would be trying to concentrate over an important golf shot when the most random thought would come into my head. Where did it come from? Why did it come to me at that moment? What should I do about it?

Guess where the blame fell if the ball didn't go where I wanted it to.

If you, too, are labouring under the misunderstanding that controlling your thoughts is desirable, or even possible, now might be a good time to check in with your direct experience. Does that belief hold true?

Try to sit for a minute and think of nothing. Or choose one thought and think it exclusively. How did you get on?

Most people believe that their perception of the world is like a video camera. That their mind is constantly producing an accurate representation of reality. This isn't true. A better analogy might be to compare perception to the world's best special-effects department. It is constantly producing a real-time projection of a material world, based on complex and incomplete information coming to us via our senses.

Therefore, we make mistakes such as misreading putts. Or we misjudge the distance to the pin because a clever course designer has placed a bunker short of the green rather than beside it. Or we wave and shout 'Hi!' to a friend on the next fairway before realising it's a complete stranger.

Despite knowing that we can be fooled by our perceptions, the system is so good, so realistic and seamless, that most of the time we forget perception is created internally. Thought creates an illusion of reality, rather than an accurate reproduction of something outside of us.

That we don't control thought is sometimes seen as a negative. It is anything but.

Literally anything can pop into our awareness at any moment. This is what enables us to be infinitely creative. To have life-changing insights. To develop skills in almost any field, and to experience the full range of emotions and feelings that make life rich and interesting.

The capacity to forget our 'selves' and get absorbed into an experience and live it fully, but then to realise the true nature of that experience not as something that happened to us, but something created by us, might be what makes the human experience unique.

We will explore this further in a later chapter.

We Get Lost in the Game

So, for golfers, what are the implications of better understanding the way thought works? How might we benefit from seeing more clearly the way our experience is created?

Let's say the thought occurs that your swing or putting isn't good enough. Something is letting you down and you need to change it. Perhaps another player has become successful, and you think you should make your golf swing more like theirs. You take the thought seriously. Feeling comes with that thinking; doubt, inadequacy or lack of confidence.

When we forget that our experience is created via thought, we become convinced that our perception of reality is the 'correct' one. We react to the situation, believing it to be real, without considering that another perspective might become available at any moment.

I can't tell you how many times I have set off down a long and frustrating road of changing or fixing something in my game because I took my insecure thinking seriously.

It wasn't a swing change that would have been helpful to me. It was a better understanding of the nature of perception.

When we forget that our perception of reality is created afresh from moment to moment, we believe that our feelings are telling us something important about the situation or circumstance.

Thought generates the experience of a situation, and it seems that we are part of that experience. It looks like our feelings are coming from outside, from what is happening to us or around us.

From ignorance, the natural response to these feelings is to try to change something. To fix the apparent cause of those feelings. Or to try to fix ourselves, which is in fact the same thing because our 'self' is made of the same stuff that the situation is made from—thought. The desire is the same, regardless. We want to feel better.

Both remedies require more thinking, which was the source of the feelings in the first place. A vicious circle is activated.

The more our thinking revs up, the stronger our feelings, and the less likely we are to remember we are thinking. And so, it goes on.

Say I'm coming down the last few holes in contention for an important tournament. If I forget the true nature of that experience – a perception within awareness rather than reality – it will look very much like my well-being depends on maintaining my position on the leader board.

If I judge that insecure or anxious feelings can hinder me in that endeavour, I might try to fix those feelings, maybe by managing my state of mind or by thinking positively. In doing so, I'm likely to make the situation worse. Employing such a strategy requires more thinking and ensures the perpetuation of the illusion.

It's Never 'Personal'

When we take something personally, we believe that what someone has said or done poses a direct threat to our happiness or wellbeing. In ignoring the nature of thought, we forget that, just as ours are, other people's views are also merely reflections of their thinking.

They behave based on their current perception of reality, which might well look very different from our own. This can be puzzling or frustrating if you don't understand.

A relationship in which two people continue to believe strongly that their different thought-created versions of reality is the 'correct' one, is unlikely to be happy or enduring.

If just one of the two sees the nature of the thought-feeling connection, that relationship will be transformed. If one sees through the illusion and doesn't react when the other person gets caught up, then the situation is less likely to escalate.

For example, when a golfer has forgotten the true nature of experience and is struggling, if a coach, caddy or partner remains clear-headed, the golfer will sense this and their thinking might well calm down.

When both people in a relationship see that their feelings ebb and flow completely independent of circumstances, including one another, that affiliation is more likely to be productive, enjoyable and long lasting.

Coming Home

If you're not enjoying your golf, it seems logical to start by looking at what motivates you to head onto the course in the first place. This is when the 'Why?' questions often start.

As I mentioned earlier, one 'Why?' question inevitably leads to another. What effect is that additional doubtful thinking likely to have on your feelings?

There is no ultimate answer to the 'Why?' question. It is an enquiry rooted in duality, in the realm of mind and matter, of cause and effect. If matter does not exist, how can cause and effect exist?

When you see this to be true, then the answer to 'why do you play golf?' is 'whatever makes sense to you in that moment'. This is the true meaning of free will. There is no right answer and no wrong one.

You might also realise that the 'Why?' question has no bearing on how you play and how much you enjoy the game. If it was really that important, would you not have had the reason clear in your mind when, as a kid, you first took up the game and fell in love with it?

For most of us, that wasn't the case. I know it wasn't for me.

The game itself is always neutral. It is what it is. How we feel about it depends 100 percent on the expectations, judgements and beliefs we have about it. We do not choose these thoughts. Therefore, we do not choose what golf means to us and why we play. It's normal and perfectly OK to love it one minute and hate it the next if that's the thinking that occurs.

Any pressure, anxiety or insecurity is a sign you have forgotten the true nature of your experience. Your feelings haven't been inflicted upon you by the game of golf or by anything else. (We will delve more deeply into true nature later in the book.)

When you see through the illusion, when you remember that who you think you are is made from the same stuff as is your perception of the game, you return to being one with it.

Golf becomes fun again, like it was when you first picked up a club and had a swing just for the hell of it, rather than for what you thought the game might do for you.

You come home.

CHAPTER 5

Myth 2—Good Golf Is Consistent Golf

WHEN A GOLFER COMES TO SEE ME for the first time, we usually have a conversation about what they are looking to achieve.

"To become more consistent" is the most common request.

Apparently, the word *consistent* means different things to different golfers. Is it a repeatable golf swing? Is it a smaller gap between best shots and worst? Is it playing to a similar standard from one game to the next?

We usually settle on something along the lines of 'playing close to your best golf most of the time.' Once we have agreed on the aspiration, we can look at taking the first steps.

If there is confusion around what consistent golf looks like, it shouldn't be a surprise that there's a prior misunderstanding to be addressed, an assumption about where consistent golf comes from. The common belief is that fixing your swing will make you a more consistent player.

Recreational golfers look at the swings and putting strokes of the best, and they believe that better swing technique is the key factor in hitting more fairways and greens. Golfers who watch the game on television or buy golf magazines are constantly bombarded with the idea that improving their golf swing is the way forward. That if they swing more like the top players do, they will play better more often.

There is an element of truth in this theory, but unfortunately, developing a move like a tour pro is not a realistic proposition for the golfer who sits behind a desk or in a car five days a week.

Few have either the time, or the physical capability to build and refine a swing like that of Justin Rose, Adam Scott or Anne van Dam. Today's top golfers are as fit and strong as any other professional athletes. They spend hours in the gym working on their power, speed and mobility. Few recreational golfers are capable of moving their bodies or golf clubs like the game's elite.

Taking lessons and practising with the goal of emulating a tour player is a worthy pursuit, but unless you are also following a similar fitness regime, you are spending time and money chasing the impossible.

If you enjoy the process, then by all means, carry on.

But is it the most efficient use of limited resources if consistent golf is what you're after?

Ever Tried To Change Your Golf Swing?

A big frustration for many club golfers is the disparity in their results from one game to the next. One weekend they play close to their handicap. The next, they are 12 shots worse. After the round, their golf swing usually gets the blame for the loss of form.

Anyone who has made major changes to their golf swing knows the difficulty of altering a long-established pattern of movement. Our beliefs and our experience contradict one another. We suspect our inconsistent play comes from the fact that our swing is different from one week to the next.

On the other hand, if you ask someone taking lessons whether the adjustment was easy, the vast majority would say no.

I've spent the last 10 years assisting golfers who hit thousands of balls in an effort to fix or improve their golf swing. To me, it makes no sense to blame a poor round on a movement that was functional a week earlier.

So, what element of your experience does change from week to week, day to day, and indeed moment to moment? And what is consistent? What never varies? If your goal is to lessen that variability, would it not make sense to explore your experience to find out what stays the same, and what fluctuates?

It is the *knowing* of your experience that is constant. You are always aware. The *content* of that experience is always changing, always in flux. We live in an ever-changing flow of thinking, feeling, sensing and perceiving.

This might explain why your golf swing feels different from day to day, week to week, but looks the same when you see it on video. The movement is fundamentally the same, but your perception of it is different. Trying to change a pattern of behaviour (your golf swing) without understanding the thinking and feeling that underpin that behaviour is liable to make things worse, not better.

So, what's going on with the golfer who plays well one week but not the next? I would suggest that in the first instance they just went out and played with freedom. No expectations. No attempts to resist or manipulate the experience. They just went with the flow.

The following week, they were cluttered, busy with comparisons between the previous experience and the current one. Judgements are made and actions are taken. This is completely normal and inevitable. Not a problem if you understand what is going on. Unfortunately, if you do not know, and you resist or try to fix your experience, there can be consequences.

Confidence, creativity, resilience and high performance are the natural by-products of a clear mind. These by-products are obscured by insecure or doubtful thinking. These thoughts manifest physically as tension or anxiety. These feelings can have a detrimental effect on the rhythm and timing of the golf swing.

Variations in timing will cause large inconsistencies in both the distance and direction of your shots.

When we act from a clear mind, we are at ease with our thinking and fluent in our movements. Every golfer knows the feeling of flow, perhaps when playing a few holes in the evening, or on the range hitting a few balls to warm up. You aren't trying. The swing feels easy, and the ball comes out of the middle of the club time after time.

In trying to swing like you did last week, or in

comparing your score with how you think you should be doing at a particular stage of the round, you are getting in your own way.

It seems to me that playing the best golf you can comes more from understanding yourself and less from having a textbook golf swing.

After all, even Adam Scott and Justin Rose sometimes shoot a score well above their average. And over the years there have been many golfers with unconventional actions who proved to be remarkably consistent competitors.

What Are You Sure Of?

As golfers, we are drawn to the idea of certainty. To the belief that if we can just get our technique right, we can somehow know what will happen when we make a swing or hit a putt.

Therefore, most golfers practice by attempting to hit shot after shot with the same club, the same flight, the same trajectory, the same result. But this isn't how we play golf. And as we noted in Chapter 2, we also have a desire to be challenged. The practice range is the only place where we can accurately compare consecutive shots.

Could the reason most golfers practice like this be because they find it very difficult to hit one shot after another in the same direction with the same ball flight? The concurrent desire for certainty and for challenge is an addictive mix for golfers and highly profitable for driving ranges and golf instructors.

If you read golf magazines or watch online instruction videos, it's easy to fall into the belief that the desire for certainty will be sated by having a repeatable golf swing. That fixing your swing will give you the feeling that you know where the ball is going to go every time. The feeling of confidence, that you are in control.

Most of us are more familiar with the feelings that accompany all the thinking about what could go wrong with the swing, and about where the ball might end up.

"I've got no idea where it's going" is a familiar lament at the 19th hole of golf clubs all over the world.

Unfortunately, these expectations, this desire for certainty, is one reason why many of us find the game so difficult.

We are searching for something that only exists in memory and in imagination. It doesn't exist in the present moment, the moment in which we hit the shot.

Certainty is an aspiration promoted by golf

magazines and websites, many of which have a business model that depends on the sale of golf instruction.

As the golf coach Michael Hebron rightly states

"The great players aren't consistent. The great players are great at dealing with inconsistency". That is wisdom.

We can't be certain about anything that happens in experience, because everything we perceive as situation or circumstance is created via thought. As Albert Einstein famously said, "Reality is an illusion, albeit a rather persistent one."

Science is sometimes defined as the study of the known world. Its most sophisticated iteration, quantum physics, tells us that there are no certainties, only levels of probability. The material world as we perceive it does not exist according to the current understanding of quantum mechanics.

Apparently solid objects such as trees, buildings, cars and people are made up of particles held together by fields of energy. If this is so, what is the true nature of our experience of them?

In an article published in *The Observer* in 1934, astrologer and physicist Sir James Hopwood Jeans suggested:

"The stream of knowledge is heading towards a non-mechanical reality. The universe begins to look more like a great thought than a great machine."

Golfers have been bombarded over the past 40 years with the suggestion that the answers to all their desires will be found in science and technology. Why, then, do most equipment companies spend far more on marketing than they spend on research and design?

As with all consumer-driven enterprises, reinforcing the belief that happiness will be found in objects and attainment is at the core of their business model. The science is just a tool to bolster that belief. People get that marketing is marketing, but they believe science to be the truth.

The line between marketing and scientific research is often blurred. Both are perceptions. Ultimately, they are different flavours of the same illusion. When golfers look in a more spiritual direction to understand their desires, rather than a scientific one, the materialist paradigm in which we currently live starts to look far less convincing.

The need for certainty, for security, for outcomes we can rely on is found in all aspects of our lives, not just our golf. When we believe we have found it—the right house, the right job, the right partner, the right amount of money in the bank, the right school for our children—we think we will be happy. That everything will be OK.

But there are no guarantees. People with wealth, status, good relationships and good health still have feelings of need and lack. A brief glance at the newspapers offers compelling evidence that money, fame and worldly success do not necessarily bring peace of mind and happiness.

We can be sure that our experience will continually change. So how do we proceed when we know that our perception of reality is an illusion? That even at the cutting edge of science there are no certainties, merely levels of probability?

The simple answer is: By exploring the true nature of experience. The awareness by which that ever-changing experience is known is the only constant. When in times of struggle we look to what we know will never change, we find the certainty we are looking for in the material world but have never found.

It is a question of trust. Are you going to put faith in your beliefs, which do change, or in the knowing of your direct experience, which is eternal?

Realising that you can still hit a good shot when you are feeling uncomfortable is not self-delusion.

Our experience is that we have hit good shots when we felt like we were going to hit a bad one, and vice versa. Having belief that you are going to hit a good shot is nice when it happens, but it doesn't mean that you will.

"In order to feel OK, I need to have it all figured out." Could this belief actually prolong insecure feelings by feeding a desire for control which can never be realised through the seeking of it?

The Myth of the Pre-Shot Routine

The quest for consistency has led golfers to put their faith in some strange superstitions.

None more so than the pre-shot routine. This is the name given to the ritual of pre-determined thoughts and movements made before the stroke that will apparently lead to the ball going to the target more often than when not performed.

The belief that in order to play consistent golf, you need to have a predetermined pre-shot routine is one of the most illogical concepts to which a golfer can subscribe.

Pages and pages have been written about this practice over the years. Following the 1995 publication of *Golf Is Not A Game of Perfect,* by Dr Bob Rotella, it has become almost universally accepted that in order to be successful, a golfer must approach each shot in the same way, with the same number of looks at the target, waggles of the club, etc.

Most of the world's golf professionals have such a routine. Is this due to evidence based on results or because they are following the herd? Do all these golfers play their best golf every single week?

If a pre-shot routine was a fundamental element of success and the cause of consistently good golf, wouldn't we expect to see players always playing to their potential? There should be far less variation in performance from week to week by the best players in the world—all of whom apparently follow the same routine week after week.

I have long struggled with the idea that a pre-determined routine is going to make a difference to the quality of my performance. I've hit great shots using a ritual, but I've also hit some dreadful ones.

The same is true when I haven't used one, on the practice ground, for example. Watch closely when tour players are warming up. Do they all follow the same routine as they do on the golf course?

Following a pre-determined routine makes me feel like I'm trying too hard and thinking too much. No doubt the comfort of a ritual is important and beneficial for some players in the same way they might believe that wearing lucky under-pants or carrying a special ball marker will help.

But a universal prerequisite of optimal perfor-mance? I'm not so sure.

I used a predetermined routine for most of my playing career. I was told by various coaches and sports psychologists that the key to confidence was to prepare for a shot in the same way every single time. So, I tried to do so.

I have felt calm and in control when using a routine, and I have felt nervous, anxious and insecure when using the same routine.

I remember several occasions standing over a shot worrying whether I had done my routine correctly. Was it one look at the target or two? Three waggles or four? Do the waggles come before the looks at the target, or after? Like most golfers, I rarely used my full routine when I practised. Yet in practice, I was a more consistent ball striker than when I played?

The truth is, a consistent set of thoughts and deeds prior to taking a golf shot is a *by-product* of a clear mind, not the *cause* as we are led to believe. Golfers who don't have a lot on their minds will efficiently, and in a timely manner, do what they need to do be ready to hit the shot.

They will simply prepare to swing. Nothing more, nothing less. Therefore, the preparations will be consistent in terms of time. Naturally, to an outside observer, this will look routine in the same way that making a cup of tea looks routine.

You wouldn't say, "I'm doing my 'pre-making a cup of tea' routine" as you filled the kettle and got the milk from the fridge. It's just making tea.

A sure way for golfers to find more on their minds than necessary when preparing for a shot is to try to deliberately think their way through the process rather than letting it happen instinctively.

You've done it a thousand times before. Just play.

Correlation Does Not Imply Causation

The belief that a pre-shot routine will help you play better is an example of confusing correlation with causation.

If you are a coach, or a golfer looking to improve your enjoyment of the game or your quality of play, you might consider embroidering the heading of this section onto your golf bag as a constant reminder.

It does the reputation of sports psychology no favours when research papers are published and announced as a breakthrough in our understanding of the sporting experience, only to find out that the researcher doesn't seem to understand that correlation does not imply causation.

Results are attributed to this or that factor. Conclusions are drawn and recommendations for action are made based on a relationship a 12-year-old with a modicum of common sense would question.

A study published in *The European Journal of Sports Science* in 2018 suggested that teams who sang their national anthem passionately before games were more successful.

Perhaps employing a singing coach would therefore improve performance?

For something to be the *cause* of an observed effect, the result or outcome should be identical 100 percent of the time.

If I drop a golf ball, it will head towards the ground. No exceptions. Gravity is the cause of the golf ball falling when it leaves my hand. If one time out of 100 the outcome is different, then the relationship is a correlation, not causal. Just one exception means you have identified a pattern, not found the cause.

For a pre-shot routine to be a causal element of

a successful golf shot, the success ratio when using it would need to be 100 percent. There might be a correlation between a player having a dependable routine and hitting more good golf shots. But might the consistency of the routine and the improved play be linked to something else?

It's the same misunderstanding when a golfer blames negative thoughts for the ball that lands out of bounds or deep in the woods.

A low-handicap golfer came to see me for a chat. He was struggling with his thinking on the tee. He was trying to visualise the ball going down the fairway, but thoughts of it sailing into trouble on the right kept coming into his head.

"And this is happening before every tee shot?" I asked.

"Pretty much every time I have a driver in my hand."

"OK, so what did you shoot yesterday?"

"77," he replied.

"How many balls did you hit in trouble right of the fairway?"

"Three or four, I think."

"From how many drives?"

"I hit the driver nine times."

"OK. I have some good news. Your thinking doesn't cause the ball to go right. If it did, it would happen *every* time you are having those thoughts, which you say is on every driver swing."

Golfers blaming their thinking for a bad shot is pure confirmation bias. They stand on the tee worrying about hitting the ball into trouble, then blame the thought when it goes there.

When they stand on the tee with some negative thoughts and hit a good shot, their thinking naturally moves on. They forget what they were thinking about prior to the swing.

They also forget the times when they've felt confident over the ball, but the shot goes out of bounds. Their golf swing gets the blame when that happens.

It would be helpful if golfers could let go of the belief that there is any causal relationship between the thinking they have prior to hitting the ball and where the ball ends up. There might be a correlation, but the relationship is not causal, despite what many golf psychology books would suggest. The belief that somehow we can influence the flight of a small, round, dimpled piece of plastic with our minds is fantasy. A superstition.

Another golf performance myth that can be put in the dustbin.

What Doesn't Change

If a golfer is playing well one week, but not the next, the first, the only place to look is to the true nature of experience.

Which part of your experience changes, is variable, is inconsistent, comes and goes? And which part never changes, always stays the same, is permanent, constant, invariable?

Wouldn't getting curious about this make more sense than constantly battling our thinking? We will explore the permanent, constant nature of awareness later in the book.

Gaining a deeper understanding of thought is a good start. Seeing the way thoughts come and go and how your feelings fluctuate in response is a game changer for many golfers. When you break the connection between what happens and how you feel, the veil has been lifted.

You are less troubled by the ever-changing thoughts and feelings, which are a normal, natural part of the everyday flow of life. When you understand how it works, your instincts are to go with the flow, rather than attempting to fight or control it.

The feelings of anxiety and tension that interfere with the rhythm and timing of a good golf swing are a result of a misunderstanding. Not the result of the situation or circumstances of your game. Or of your life.

Knowing this to be true is the first step on the path of reducing the gap between your best and worst shots, the path to playing your best golf more often.

CHAPTER 6

Myth 3—State of Mind Matters

THE PREVIOUS CHAPTER SUGGESTED THAT trying to become more consistent by employing a predetermined pre-shot routine can get in the way of playing creative, instinctive, free-flowing golf.

It's hard to imagine the deliberate use of a mental technique or strategy that wouldn't lead a golfer to think more. Such overthinking can impede the natural rhythm and timing of the swing.

In this chapter, we'll explore another widely held but limiting belief, the idea that in order to play your best golf, one frame of mind might be better than another.

Most golfers think that in order to play well, they need to be in a confident, calm, focused or other 'helpful' mindset. This belief leads to recurring problems.

If you are struggling with the mental side of the game, it is invariably because you are trusting a belief over your direct experience. For example, there is a marked difference between how far most recreational golfers believe they can hit the ball and how far they actually do. This gets them into trouble with club selection on holes with forced carries over water or sand.

You don't need academic research to realise that your state of mind can't guarantee that you play well or cause you to play badly. As with the example above, you can figure this out by looking more closely at your own game without the distortions of belief getting in the way.

All golfers have days where they feel anxious or low on confidence, but then surprise themselves by playing good golf. And we have all had days where we've felt great, prepared well, and anticipated a good round, but played well below expectations.

We have evidence from our own experience that state of mind has no direct bearing on performance. Yet many of the techniques and strategies suggested by coaches and psychologists are prescribed specifically to put golfers in a positive frame of mind, or to help them build confidence.

When golfers realise that they can play well even when they are feeling doubtful or insecure, they might well ask themselves whether such interventions are necessary. This insight alone can be a relief if you are under the impression that you need to feel one way rather than another when playing an important round.

Superstition or Strategy?

Once you notice and start to enjoy the peace of mind that comes with seeing the true nature of life more deeply, it's natural to want to experience it more.

This can be a tricky moment. The temptation will arise to find ways to get into feeling that way when you play. It's easy to slip back into old habits of trying to manage your thoughts and feelings. We don't control our thinking, so the misunderstanding can reassert itself.

Mental techniques or strategies are intended to help a golfer cope with a feeling, situation or circumstance. Or to attain a state that the golfer believes will assist their performance. The techniques are neutral. While a golfer may *believe* certain techniques are helpful, the truth is, for a technique or strategy to be the cause of a state of mind, it would need to have the same effect 100 percent of the time it was employed.

I don't know of any such method.

Again, confirmation bias enters the equation.

We feel confident one day, and we play well. We attribute our success to our mindset. Another day, we feel insecure and play poorly. We make the same attribution to state of mind. Pretty soon, this imagined link between feeling state and outcome becomes our reality.

A day where our bias is not confirmed is either forgotten or considered a fluke. We ignore the exception that disproves the 'rule', in favour of proving it.

A good moment to remember that *correlation does not imply causation.*

Thousands of golfers around the world willingly perpetuate the illusion that confidence can be enhanced through external objects. How? By carrying a lucky ball marker, using a favourite club for important shots, or perhaps by wearing a piece of clothing that they once played well in.

When you understand the nature of the connection between thought and feeling, you will see how and why these practices and rituals can seem to have a positive effect, but are merely superstitions. Without this understanding, however, these rituals will seem like necessities, and golfers may even experience anxiety if they are not able to perform them.

When someone wakes up to the true nature of

how experience is created, they appreciate that their best comes from who they really are, not what they do or how they do it. With this realisation, the idea of using a strategy or a technique isn't taken seriously anymore.

There is nothing that needs to be fixed or coped with. Mindset can't be improved or enhanced by employing any sort of mental tool.

It's not possible to attain a specific mental state through force of will. The key to peace of mind is not just the realisation that you can't control your thoughts and feelings. It's knowing that you never need to.

Many people experience a quiet, peaceful feeling when meditating, visualising or breathing deeply. But did the practice cause the state of mind? It's fine if you adopt any of these techniques. But if just 1 time out of 100, the improved feeling you are seeking doesn't arise, you might want to question whether you are witnessing a correlation or the cause.

In the gaps between thoughts and perceptions, pure awareness is revealed as the constant, fundamental element of our experience, and our true nature is revealed. This can happen anywhere, and at any moment. On a prayer mat, at the top of a mountain, in a forest, at a busy Tube station, on a golf course, or at your office desk.

Your true nature is witnessed as presence, happiness, love, or simply being.

It's what you have been seeking all along.

The Power of Insight

Unfortunately, just reading words on a page won't lead to a deeper level of understanding. Intellectual knowledge is not the same as realising something somatically. Realisation appears in the form of insight, and it is felt at a deeper level.

Insight prevails when personal thinking drops away. When we get quiet, when we find ourselves falling into the stillness beyond thought.

Remember a time in your life when you truly 'got' something for the first time. When you learned to walk, to speak, to play a musical instrument, to do quadratic equations, to use a computer, to swing a golf club—you had insights. You had deep realisations about your experience.

An insight can happen at any time. Hopefully, you will have many insights about your golf over the coming weeks and months. Your game is pure potential just waiting to be realised. Insights come into the world via you. Great golf shots are created through you.

Would they and the world they appear in exist if you don't exist? A question we will explore later.

When you have an insight, a realisation, it might seem very ordinary. You see the implications of a principle. You have stripped away complexity to reveal an idea or concept in a simpler form. We have all had the experience of figuring something out then wondering how the answer had eluded us for so long.

To recall what we learned in an earlier chapter, a principle is a piece of knowledge that is true, that you can count on. It's something you can trust, something you can rely on completely. From principles, we derive implications. An implication is an explanation of how something works in the world of form, based on a principle.

As mentioned earlier, Sir Isaac Newton's laws are principles of physics. From these principles, implications are derived that can be seen in everyday life. They are all around us. In the buildings we live in, the bridges beneath our feet, the aeroplanes flying above our heads.

Knowing for certain that a feeling is not directly caused by circumstances will have implications for a golfer who feels anxious and insecure coming down the last few holes of a tournament with a slender lead.

If the golfer believes that the unwanted feelings are coming from their standing in the tournament, the obvious remedy is to get out of that situation. To do something to change the circumstances that are responsible for the feelings.

The easiest way for the ego to protect itself, to relieve the pressure, would be to interfere with a couple of swings so that shots are dropped and the golfer is no longer in contention. On a conscious level, this is the last thing the golfer wants. But because we don't control thoughts, feelings or actions in the way we like to think we do, it might well be how the end of their tournament plays out.

Which points us to another myth that we'll explore in the next chapter. If we were in control of thought and deed, how could such an act of self-sabotage occur?

With the dropped shots, the golfer slips down the leader board. The tension evaporates, replaced by feelings of regret, frustration or despair.

The experience of getting in your own way like this might be familiar. Things are going along nicely, and then, suddenly, you get nervous and play a couple of bad holes. Afterwards, you wonder what happened. If you look outwards to the world of form, you might blame your golf swing or a lack of 'mental toughness' for the reversal.

Rarely is the true reason uncovered.

A golfer who understands that they are just feeling the energy of their thinking in the moment has no reason to want to fix those feelings, or to change the situation. They know that feelings can't prevent them hitting the shots they want to hit.

This golfer is less likely to self-sabotage, and more likely to enjoy the experience of being in contention.

Insights often occur when we question something we thought we knew. Something we took for granted. Hopefully, this book will encourage you to entertain some new and different questions regarding your golf and your beliefs about it. Self-enquiry is the direct path to realisation.

Sometimes an insight occurs when your coach tells a story or offers metaphors to illustrate a theory or idea. The words are intended to trigger something associated with your experience that inspires a different perspective. That stimulates some fresh thinking about your golf or another area of your life.

Learning does not come from the teacher. It can only ever come from within the learner.

The examples in this book are intended to point

towards true nature. To allow a glimpse past thoughts, feelings and perceptions. To sense something beyond what you think of as 'you'.

There is nothing to learn, practice, or apply as a method or strategy in order to attain a state of mind.

If an insight about the nature of experience arises, your understanding of how life works will be deeper. The attraction of techniques or strategies will fade. The quiet state of awareness will be felt more often.

More insights will flow, and so it goes on.

True Nature

I sometimes get asked how my understanding has developed since the previous book was published in March 2016. Most significant has been a deeper appreciation of the primary nature of awareness, or consciousness.

In many spiritual traditions, the experience of knowing, or of being aware, is referred to as consciousness. In this context, the words *awareness* and *consciousness* are interchangeable.

I sensed the relevance of awareness to a golfer when I wrote about it in Chapter 6 of *The Three Principles of Outstanding Golf*. But I underestimated its significance.

Consciousness is the fundamental element of all experience. It's how we know that we know. It is primary. The ultimate. The one true reality.

I still think the suggestions made previously might be useful to a golfer. Becoming more aware of what is happening, rather than thinking too much about what you should or shouldn't be doing, can be useful.

But implying that awareness is a doing—an action—was misguided. It suggests that awareness is personal. Something that belongs to us and that we have control over. This isn't the case.

Awareness is what all experience, including that of who we think we are, arises from. The source. It is our fundamental state of being. It's not a doing. It is shared with every other aware being.

When coaching or advising, pointing to the personal, suggesting there is something to do or not do, is rarely helpful. That I did so previously is a regret. Making it personal just takes someone into their mind. Into the content of experience. That isn't where wisdom is found. To understand who we really are, we need to go beyond thought to what is universal. To the knowing of experience.

It is more helpful to point to what is true in

every human experience. In so doing, truth can be seen. Seeking ends. Insight can occur, and the right course of action in that moment becomes apparent.

Consciousness, or awareness, is the fundamental, universal element of experience. It is the only constant. Awareness is the same for, and shared by, everyone and everything. Try to find an edge, a limit to awareness? If there is no point at which my awareness ends and becomes your awareness, it must be one?

Our thoughts, feelings, sensations and perceptions change moment to moment. They are unique to the perceiver. But awareness, in which all of those arise and disappear, is ever-present.

It is ubiquitous.

The awareness of life and golf now, at this moment, is the same awareness as when you first picked up a club all those years ago. Awareness will be the same when you hit your last putt as it is today.

The consciousness of which I am aware is the same as the consciousness that is experienced by every other aware being. Another word for consciousness is *knowing*. Every living creature knows. What they know is unique, but knowing is universal.

All major religions and philosophies have at their core the tenet that all men and women are created equal. They are calling attention to a universal consciousness. The knowing or awareness of being. What every person is referring to when they say "I am".

There are no levels of consciousness. Awareness is constant, permanent, eternal and unchanging. When we talk about high or low states of mind, or levels of consciousness, what we are really pointing to are varying levels of personal thinking.

Thinking obscures awareness, and our mood descends. That thinking moves on, awareness is revealed, and our mood rises. Consciousness itself does not change. It is the degree to which our thinking veils it that ebbs and flows.

Are You Aware?

As well as allowing us to be aware of what we are thinking, consciousness allows us to be aware *that* we think.

We cannot think of, perceive, sense or know anything outside awareness. Have you ever had an experience that you weren't aware of? How would you know about it?

Asking the question "Am I aware?" is a simple

way to begin an enquiry into the true nature of our experience. Try it now. What happens?

The first time you consider the question, you might be distracted by the content of experience. Many people respond with a question:

"Aware of what?"

If you ignore the 'what' you might get an intuition that the nature of our experience is different from what we believe it to be. It comes when we glimpse a separation between the *content* of experience—objects, whether thoughts or perceptions—and the awareness *of* experience. In the gap between thoughts, we become aware of awareness itself.

We have the capacity to go beyond personal thought, to realise that whatever it is that allows us to know that we are thinking never leaves. The more we see that there is a distinction between the *knowing* of our experience—who we really are— and the *content* of that experience—the ego and its story—the less likely we are to be disturbed by our thoughts, feelings and perceptions.

Understanding the nature of experience allows us to see how and why our mood or state of mind can rise in an instant. We see that our feelings aren't caused by what is happening to us or around us. We realise the innocence of the mistake, and it feels like a weight has been lifted.

Ignorance, in this context, does not mean stupidity. It just describes a state where we forget who we are. Content and the knowing of it merge. We become lost in the story or in the meaning we have attached to a situation. We take our thinking seriously, and life suddenly seems bleak or troubling. Golf becomes joyless and hard work.

When you are feeling isolated, anxious and insecure; when your mood is low, ask yourself: "Am I aware?" In that moment, between awareness of the question and knowing the answer, what happens to your troubles?

When you think about a problem in your golf, ask, "To whom does this matter?" Is the awareness of a good day on the course any different from the awareness of a bad day? The experience is different, but awareness is the same.

You might see that you are not your thoughts. You are not the story being told about your life. You are not the central character in that story. You are what knows the story. The witnessing presence.

You are awareness of thoughts and feelings, of body and mind.

In ignorance, the feelings of peace and love for

life, of happiness, which are implicit in pure awareness, become veiled by thought. The ego, our personal self—who we believe we are—becomes our dominant perspective on reality.

This illusory entity becomes blind to the knowing of its own being—to the awareness from which it arose—and assumes itself separate. The separate self (ego) is infinite consciousness to which a limit has been applied. This limiting, this separation from source, is the cause of the longing and seeking with which all human beings are familiar.

The ego then attempts to satisfy this longing in objects, relationships or activities such as golf, business and other games.

The ego itself only appears as an entity. It is an activity of consciousness.

Happiness Is Who We Really Are

We all have a memory of the peace, happiness, love and freedom that is our true nature. We all know what happiness feels like. If we didn't know it and value it, why would we seek it or have the desire to find it again?

This desire, this wanting, is felt by most golfers as motivation to compete, to improve, to succeed. There is nothing wrong with any of these feelings. They are normal and healthy. The misunderstanding occurs when we achieve a goal and think we have 'found' happiness in that achievement.

To the contrary, however, happiness was always there, like the sun behind the clouds. In achieving the goal, we stopped wanting and seeking for a while, the clouds drifted away, allowing us to feel the peace and fulfilment of true nature.

Everything the separate self does is an effort to cast off the limitations that created it in the first place through our personal thinking, to return to the peace and happiness of the knowing of its source.

If the ego attempts this from a misunderstanding of the true nature of its own being, it will look for happiness in the outside world. It will believe its happiness came from a golf shot, from the outcome of a match or tournament, or from a handicap reduction or a ranking on an Order of Merit.

When one of these external circumstances aligns with the thinking about it, the desiring of it and the seeking stops. Freedom, peace and happiness are experienced once more.

Unfortunately, the separate self imagines a causal relationship between the feeling of happiness and the event. It assumes responsibility for the success and the feelings. A feedback loop is created. When the good feelings subside, as they always do, the striving resumes. The search for the next achievement begins.

When we realise that happiness *is* true nature, that the peace and love and contentment that we seek are always available to us as the knowing of our true being, the quest is over.

We go back to playing games such as golf for the same reasons we did when we were children, rather than attaching meaning to them.

We just play because we can. The game resumes as an expression *of* happiness rather than a route *to* happiness. When this becomes clear, we are free.

Understanding more deeply the nature of being has been the biggest step forward on the journey— even more so than realising the relationship between thought and feeling and seeing that my state of mind had nothing to do with my life circumstances.

As I now see it, awareness isn't something we do. It's who we really are.

For many golfers, seeing the nature of thought is a game changer in understanding how they feel from moment to moment on and off the golf course. But understanding the true nature of who you really are offers a depth of wellbeing which goes far beyond the daily ups and downs.

It can't really be put into words. Realising the true nature of our experience is what the whole game of life, including golf, is about.

CHAPTER 7

Myth 4—Control the Controllables

OVER THE PAST FOUR DECADES, it has become widely recognised that learning about the way we think and feel on the course can have an impact on golfing performance.

We often hear coaches and commentators express concepts and use phrases that point to the way they think a golfer's mind works. On the surface, many of these ideas seem plausible.

For example, we often hear that in order to be successful, a golfer needs to 'control the controllables.'

The suggestion is that our internal environment should be regulated. We should monitor our state of mind and manage our motivation, willpower, concentration, focus and desire to suit the situation or circumstance.

At the same time, golfers should neither think about nor dwell upon things that are outside their control—the opposition, the golf course, playing partners, the conditions of the playing environment, or the weather.

From a limited understanding of the nature of experience, this seems reasonable.

But can it really be as simple as choosing what sort of thoughts and feelings you want to be in from moment to moment?

If that were possible, wouldn't we all be happier, more confident, more motivated, more focused and more positive all our lives? If we really could choose our state of mind, wouldn't the performance coaches and sports psychologists who are suggesting how we should do this, be redundant?

At any given moment, there are thousands of biological and chemical processes taking place in the body. Blood is pumping through arteries and veins. Cells are dying and being replaced. Food is being digested and used for energy. Perceptions are being formed from the information arriving via our senses and analysed by the brain and nervous system. Decisions are made, and actions take place based on these perceptions.

These bodily functions just continue without us even being aware they are happening. We don't exercise agency or conscious control over them. But curiously, for some reason, we have come to believe that there are a few exceptions to this rule, namely our thinking, our feelings and our moods.

What makes these activities different? Isn't that a bit strange?

And if we aren't in control of what we think, feel and perceive, can we say we are truly in control of our actions and behaviour? After all, we can only act on a thought that occurs to us. If we don't think about something, if it isn't part of our experience, for all intents and purposes it doesn't exist.

Is Thinking A 'Controllable'?

One thing that drew me to golf as a teenager was the belief that I was wholly responsible for my success or failure; for how I played, whether I won or lost.

Before I got serious about the game, I played mainly team sports. It was frustrating when I played well but the team lost, especially if I felt my teammates weren't matching my levels of effort and commitment. And if I played poorly but still ended up on the winning team, the victory felt hollow.

Golf didn't have these contradictions. If I played well as an individual, I was successful; if I played badly, I wasn't. To a young man trying to make sense of how the world worked, this seemed logical, reasonable and fair.

Looking back, it was around this time that I lost my way. I was at an age where I was trying to work out who I thought I was and what my purpose in life might be. Like many teenagers, I wanted my independence. Playing a game where I seemed to be in control of my own destiny fit this mindset more than one where I relied on others.

So, I gave up team sports and golf became the major distraction from my studies.

This belief that I had to be in control of my game, my success or failure, and therefore my happiness, persisted until my late 30s. It's perhaps the main reason why I felt overwhelmed and never became the golfer I thought I could have been.

Once I became a competent striker of the ball, I spent most of my playing career trying to understand, regulate and manage my thinking, both on and off the golf course.

The players who were beating me weren't all hitting shots that were way better than mine. So, I surmised that something they were doing on the mental side of the game must have been making the difference. I was as intelligent and well educated as most of them, so I resolved to work as hard on my thinking as I did on my driving, iron play and putting.

It was a constant effort monitoring what was coming and going from awareness. I kept reams of notes about what I thought and felt when playing or practising. My yardage books were filled with scribblings of things to think or not to think on the course.

I spent hours evaluating whether the thoughts that came to me were helpful or harmful, what they might mean, and then trying to either accentuate the positive or eliminate the negative.

Anyone who has read about sports psychology or listened to golf commentary might well be under the impression that this is what good players do.

Apparently, they think positively, replace negative thoughts with positive ones, make good decisions, have self-confidence and generally keep their mental state under conscious control.

Is this really the case?

Many of the players I competed against were following similar strategies. Those strategies haven't moved on in the last 20 years.

Let's say there are 150 golfers in a tournament, and most of them think positively, control their mindset and visualise good shots. Only 70 of those golfers will make the cut, and one will take home the trophy. Different golfers play well from week to week. Therefore, the evidence would suggest that the preferred mental model of top professional golfers is more of a superstition than a definitive element of performance.

In my experience, human beings do not have the power or capacity to control what thoughts they think or when they think them.

This was a big challenge to my ego when I first heard this. I strongly disagreed. I wanted to feel that I was responsible for my results. If I wasn't, how could I take the credit and enjoy the feelings when I was successful? Initially, I preferred my beliefs to what my experience was telling me.

But as I looked more closely at the evidence of my own thoughts and feelings, I realised that it was true. I couldn't control my thinking. Random thoughts popped into awareness all the time. Sometimes, despite my best efforts I couldn't stop thinking about a tough shot coming up later in the round, or a bad break that had happened earlier.

Belief and years of conditioning were telling me I should think more positively. Eliminate the 'bad' thoughts. Visualise success, and it would follow. But my experience was telling me that the strategy wasn't working. My map of how my mental processes operated was deeply flawed.

As mentioned earlier, this idea that we can be in control of ourselves, of our swing and, by proxy, of our golf ball, is seductive.

It is an illusion, albeit a persistent and attractive one. Most golfers would very much like it to be true. Any time that we put our faith in an illusion, especially one we don't understand, suffering tends to follow.

Can You Choose To Be Happy?

When I ask people what aspect of golf is most important to them, most say enjoyment. Golf does not exist in isolation. It is part of a bigger picture. If you grant someone a single wish, invariably they say, "I want to be happy." The seeking of enjoyment from golf is a proxy for seeking happiness in life.

If we are truly in control of our thinking, and our feelings come from thought, then happiness and enjoyment would be a given. We would just choose the thought that says, "I'm truly OK with everything that is happening around me in my life and on the golf course right now. Nothing is lacking." A feeling of contentment would follow immediately.

Hit a snap hook into a pond? Just choose the

thought, "I'm fine with that."

Hit a big slice out of bounds? Choose a thought along the lines of, "No problem, I didn't like that golf ball anyway."

Three-putt the 72nd green to lose a Major Championship? Just think, "That's OK, I didn't want all the media attention."

I'm sure you can think of situations from the past that might cause you to question the theory that we can choose what we think about and therefore choose how we feel. Despite this evidence, golfers are told, "You may not be able to control what happens, but you can control your response to what happens."

Really? Is that honestly true in your experience? I'm pretty sure I just think what I think when I think it. If, after missing a putt, I have the thought, "Throw the putter into the lake", the club will be airborne and there will be a splash unless I have a subsequent thought that says, "That isn't a good idea."

And if we don't control our thinking, do we control our golf swing?

And if we don't control our golf swing, do we control our golf ball?

These questions point us to why the game frustrates and fascinates in equal measure. As described in Chapter 2, we love the challenge inherent in mastering something that is nigh on impossible to master.

If we could control our thinking, we would always be in total control of our body. We would always be in control of the golf club, and therefore the ball. We would shoot sub-60 every time we went out to play, and golf would be about as interesting as mowing the lawn.

We don't enjoy our golf when we are of the opinion that something is lacking. Other areas of life are a struggle because we often have a lot of thinking going on that says, "I don't really like what is happening right now. I really wish things were different."

We don't choose that sort of thinking. It just comes to us sometimes. There is nothing we can do to prevent it. The only way to cope with it or fix it is with more thinking.

The good news is, we don't need to do either. Left alone, it will pass.

It Is What It Is

When we recognise thought for what it is—an experience—rather than what we believe it to be—reality—it loses much of its power to affect our feelings.

For many people, this idea that we have no control, no personal responsibility, no agency is troubling. The question that follows is usually along the lines of:

"Well, if I'm not in control, what or who is?" The subtext of that question is:

"And who gets the credit when things go well, or the blame when they don't?"

The idea that there must be some sort of design, some grand plan—that someone or something is pulling the strings if we aren't—is a hard one to ignore. Before we address that question, let me offer a few more examples of how our thinking goes astray.

Some situations that might sound familiar:

You are at a meeting or gathering. Someone you have met previously comes over to say hello.

As they approach, it suddenly dawns on you that despite having met them before and knowing who they are, you cannot in that moment, recall their name.

How could this happen if we can choose what we think about?

*   *   *

You are having a conversation with someone at the office.

Suddenly you have great idea about a project you are working on.

The conversation continues, and you try to pay attention to what the other person is saying while at the same time trying to remember the great insight that just came to you.

By the time you get back to your desk it has gone. You try to retrace your mental steps to recall what it was, but all you can remember is the conversation.

Later that afternoon on the journey home, it comes back.

Thankfully, you have the chance to pull over and write it down.

Still think you are in control of what you think about and when you think it?

*   *   *

You are cooking a special meal at home. You go to the pantry only to find you have run out of a vital ingredient. You grab your keys, jump in the car and dash to the shops.

As you pick up a shopping basket, you notice a special offer on desserts in the first aisle. You remember you need milk for breakfast in the morning and that you are running low on dog food.

You throw everything into your basket, pay at the till and then head back to the house to finish cooking.

You unload the bag only to find that you have forgotten to purchase the key ingredient you went to the shop for in the first place.

Time and again, we hear coaches and sports psychologists tell us we should be trying to 'control the controllables', and that these 'controllables' include our thinking, feelings, emotions, perceptions and other mental processes.

Look closely at your experience. Is this possible? If we did have agency over thought, we would never lose anything, never forget anything and never make a poor choice or bad decision. While that sounds tempting, there would be a heavy price to pay.

If we controlled thought, we could never have an insight or a creative idea that solves a problem.

Never have a flash of inspiration that thrilled and excited us. Never be pleasantly surprised by our own ingenuity. We could never create anything beyond what we already know or might learn from someone else.

The greatest discoveries in human history would never have happened if all we could ever think was what was already stored in our intellect. How could you choose a thought if you didn't already know about it? If we controlled thought, we'd essentially be clever robots.

The capacity for insight, for fresh new thinking to spring from wherever it does, is one of the things that makes life such an amazing experience. A thought comes to us, takes form in awareness, then dissipates. This process is happening every moment we are alive.

We can't stop it or control it. The good news is we don't need to. Nor would we want to.

As I have said previously, please don't take my word for it. Explore your own experience before accepting or rejecting it. If you see that this is indeed the case, the implications for your life could be profound.

The fact that we don't control thought hasn't just suddenly become true because you read these words.

The world didn't suddenly go from being flat to being round when Pythagoras had his insight 2000 years ago. And your control over thinking and feeling hasn't just ended with the realisation that, in fact, you don't have any.

It has always been the case.

Everything that you have ever achieved or accomplished in your life has been without conscious control of your thoughts and feelings. Whatever the circumstances of your life up to this point, you have ended up here and now without choosing any of it. Life is playing out in the only way it can.

This is true for everyone. Always has been, always will be.

It brings us back to the question, "if I am not in control, who or what is?" It's a big question. The biggest one of all. A question people have been asking for thousands of years.

Who am I, and what is the nature of my existence?

The answer lies in understanding the true nature of experience. That there is one fundamental reality, and that reality is consciousness. There is not more than one.

There is no evidence for a controller or controlled. Mind and matter are perceptions. There is no ultimate cause, and therefore there are no effects. Time and space are relative concepts, not principles.

If we trust our experience rather than belief, the fundamental nature of reality is simply awareness, presence, oneness, consciousness, being.

The separate self or ego, the one who worries about control, is a thought. A refraction of the infinite consciousness or awareness from which our entire experience is derived and in which it takes place. When we come to see that this is true, any worries about who or what is in control seem trivial, irrelevant even.

This is the ultimate freedom, a feeling we all know, love and cherish.

To give up any notion of control, and therefore of becoming, is to live a life of love and fulfilment. We are already enough. To understand that it is possible to be happy without struggling, grinding and controlling is the greatest gift. Remembering our true nature helps us be kinder to ourselves and others when the vagaries of our thinking take us in a different direction from the one we thought we might have wanted.

'Growth Mindset'

Over the past few years, the theory that human

beings need to be in a particular state of mind—the proper *mindset*—in order to learn and develop has become common currency.

(We will address learning in more detail in chapter 9.)

The term 'growth mindset' was popularised by Carol Dweck in her book *Mindset*, first published in 2006.

As Dweck herself states, mindset is a belief, a thought. Unfortunately, many people seem to have misunderstood this and taken it to mean something more tangible. A place from where thoughts, feelings and ideas arise.

In truth, 'growth mindset' is just a label given to the innate human capacity to learn continually. No one needs to find it, grow it, acquire it, develop it, teach it, practice it or even know they have it. It's part of who we are.

We have had an unlimited capacity for learning for the entire 200,000 years of our existence. We can't lose it. It's part of true nature.

Here is an example of a situation we have probably all encountered.

At some point in our lives, we have all put our hand on something hot, maybe picked up a pan or a dish that has just come out of the oven.

The first time we did it, we were probably quite young.

The pain we felt was an important lesson. We probably didn't repeat our mistake again for some time afterwards.

It is instructive that we didn't need to *do anything* beyond the encounter itself in order to learn that putting a hand on a hot dish is not a good idea. We didn't need to be in a 'growth mindset.'

We didn't need to read a book, watch a video or go on a training course for our future behaviour to change.

We became aware of an important implication of the principle of thermodynamics. Touching a hot object causes pain. We realised that contact with high temperatures should be avoided. This insight, understanding, realisation inspired our behaviour to change as we carried on with life.

Now, this doesn't mean that at some point since we haven't made the same mistake again.

Maybe we didn't realise that the object we picked up was hot, or perhaps, more likely, we were distracted, thinking about something else. Does this mean that we need to learn about not touching hot things all over again?

Of course not. Once you know something, you

know it. Even though you forget. Even when your mind is on another train of thought and not on the matter at hand, you still know it.

Now that we understand the nature of thought—the fact that we don't control it, the fact that it ebbs and flows—we see that forgetting is as normal as remembering.

Mistakes and misjudgements happen. We get lost in thought. We drift away into memories of the past, or imaginings of the future. The present moment passes us by. If we don't see it as a problem, we don't seek a solution. We don't put fuel on the fire.

The less we try to control our thinking, the more we respect the way our inner wisdom and common sense can guide us, the less we get in our own way. We can trust that we have the potential to learn what we need to learn when we need to learn it without the need for preparation or conscious control.

We don't need to fix or alter our state of mind for learning to take place. The more we see that this is true, the more we allow our behaviour to change and adapt naturally and without effort.

We can stop worrying and overthinking. We can let our innate capacity for insight move us forward. Developing our talent becomes simpler and more enjoyable. This might take the form of playing more and practising less.

Allow me to point you back to something you have experienced earlier in your life and may have observed in the life of someone close to you.

We did most of our learning when we were children, particularly when it came to motor skills and movement. How did this learning take place? By reading books? Watching videos? Going to classes?

I'd imagine not. You probably learned as I did, by playing. By trial and error. By doing.

If you have youngsters of your own, you might have watched with wonder as they quickly figured out how they could have the most fun with a new toy or game.

It might not be the way the game was intended to work, but if left alone, kids just find a way to enjoy it. This capacity to figure it out is built in. It's part of the system. It's the reason we are always evolving and adapting.

The flaw in the arrangement is the fact that we forget the nature of thought and try to override a system that works beautifully all on its own. The only lesson we need is to keep our fingers out of the machinery and to let learning come to us, rather than chasing it and trying to control or force it.

We don't need to learn how to learn, nor do we need to manage or manipulate our state of mind in order to make learning happen.

Learning is as much a part of who we are as breathing.

CHAPTER 8

Myth 5—Hard Work Ensures Success

I REGULARLY SPEAK TO GOLFERS about their game. Many work hard trying to improve. The feedback from golfers who have collectively spent hundreds of hours on the driving range and have hit tens of thousands of golf balls is telling.

Unfortunately, when they get out onto the golf course, many of them aren't seeing the improvement their efforts suggest they might expect.

Golfers are understandably frustrated that hours spent perfecting their swing technique, pounding out miles on the running machine and holing yards of putts on the practice green, isn't necessarily translating into lower scores or more enjoyable golf.

If the answers were to be found in the physical world, it's a surprise we haven't found them by now considering all the endeavour.

As it becomes more apparent that beating balls can only take you so far, many golfers are getting curious about other possibilities. What is the true nature of the relationship between mind and matter? How might this relationship affect their performance and enjoyment of the game on which they spend so much time and money.

They're disillusioned by the diminishing returns from digging the dirt on the practice range, from grinding away on the putting green and in the gym, from mainly thinking about the technical side of the game. They're ready to look in a different direction.

As they come to this point, however, it is far from obvious where they should start. Many golfers have read books or articles that promise to help them think better on the golf course, to become more resilient, to make better decisions.

They implement the strategies and techniques that are suggested. They work harder at the mental side of the game. They will themselves to focus, to relax, to be more confident, to commit, to have a better attitude, to never give up.

They might see an upturn in form as old patterns of thinking drop away, but new ones soon take their place. Constantly monitoring and pushing oneself is exhausting. Soon they find themselves back where they were, feeling even more resigned and frustrated than before. At the end of another path to success that turned out to be a dead end.

Another false dawn comes and goes. Another plausible idea that turned out pretty much the same as the last one. No wonder golfers are sceptical. No wonder they fall back on the tried and tested formula of ball bashing and grinding, doing what everyone else seems to be doing, despite the slow progress and limited returns.

At least they feel like they are investing in something tangible. They can measure their commitment in hours spent or the number of balls hit. They might even get a few compliments from people who notice the time and effort they are putting in. But this is cold comfort when you look back at the end of the season to find your handicap in the same place as when it started.

If You Do What You've Always Done ...

You'll get what you've always got—as the old saying goes.

Here's a different idea.

It might come as a surprise that I'm not suggesting you 'work' for even one second at the mental side of your game. You don't need to work on your mind any more than you need to work on digesting the sandwich you had for lunch, or on the way your heart pumps blood around your body.

An innate intelligence is constantly at play. 'You' do not exist, let alone take action in the world of form, without psychological activity taking place. The process isn't broken, and it doesn't need fixing or improving. What might be helpful is to get a better understanding of how it works.

Misunderstanding why we feel the way we feel about golf is a trap we all fall into. If we don't understand the nature of our experience—of who we really are—how can we hope to make sense of the content of our experience, of what we think of as reality?

Imagine you read somewhere that if you started breathing heavily and your heartbeat rose higher than normal, it meant you were ill and could possibly die. Every time you climbed a flight of stairs or ran for the bus you would be worried, anxious and insecure about what might happen.

Pretty soon you would manage life in such a way that you never exerted yourself. You would avoid situations where you had to do physical exercise. Far from doing you good and keeping you healthy, this misunderstanding would actually be harming you.

Gradually you would lose fitness, and your health would deteriorate. All because you read some inaccurate information and, innocently, you took it seriously.

This is what has happened with our understanding of how our minds work. We misunderstand the information our feelings are providing. We think they are telling us something about the world, something about 'out there'. They are actually prompting us to enquire as to the nature of what is experiencing the feelings.

They are pointing us inwards. Not outwards.

Understanding Doesn't Take Work

Many golfers are wary of exploring the mental side of the game. Maybe because they have had an underwhelming experience in the past, or because they think it shows a sign of weakness. Or simply because they don't feel the need to.

Counterintuitively, this is a good thing. Wisdom is telling us that there is nothing to do, nothing to fix, nothing to work at.

When we stop striving and seeking, it allows us to see beyond the myths and misunderstandings. We can just get on with life, play our golf and let insights drive learning as we go. No monitoring, evaluating or grinding is required.

Again it's a matter of looking to the nature of experience, rather than getting caught in the content of it. Of becoming aware. Of recognising your true self and allowing life to unfold from that new perspective. Of examining your beliefs and seeing if they hold true in the light of a deeper understanding.

Let's follow the above analogy to its conclusion.

You go for a medical check-up. You tell the doctor you are feeling unfit and are worried. He asks you why, and you explain that you read about it being dangerous to elevate your heart rate and get out of breath, so you've stopped exercising.

Fortunately, he is a kind doctor who can see how concerned you are. So, he calmly explains that the information you took seriously isn't true. That, in fact, exercise is very beneficial. That getting your heart rate and breathing up is actually a good idea and will make you fitter and improve your quality of life in the long term.

Would you have to 'work' at understanding what the doctor told you? Or would you just absorb the information, abandon the erroneous belief and allow your behaviour to fall into line with your change in perspective?

Regardless of what you did from that point, I can guarantee that once your perspective changed, how you felt would change.

You would stop being worried and anxious about situations where you might have to exert yourself, and you would probably look forward to some nice long walks on the golf course.

Maybe you would renew your gym membership. Sure, you could describe it as 'working on your fitness', but really you would just be getting on with your life.

Your capacity for resilience, concentration, learning and performance under pressure is realised through insight. Not by working hard. Not by forcing yourself, struggling or enduring. By simply noticing that a different way of seeing things is available and allowing the implications of that change in perspective to show up in your golf.

No grinding or grafting required.

Is It Mental or Physical?

What happens when a golfer's mental intentions and physical preparations don't match up?

It's not unusual for a player to get to the stage where they are hitting the ball well in lessons or in practice but can't seem to take that form onto the course. In almost every case, the problem is a simple one. Their physical alignment doesn't match their perception of the intended target.

Right-handers will usually aim right of where they think they are aiming, often because this feels like a more powerful address position. This is unfortunate. First, if they do hit a solid, straight shot, the ball will finish yards from where they thought they were aimed.

But hitting a straight shot out the centre of the club will be a rare occurrence, because their mental and physical intentions don't match up. An inner conflict ensues the moment they assume their posture and stance.

Their mind is set to hit the ball one place, be it to the flag or a point in the fairway. Their body is aligned to hit it somewhere else. There is a mismatch between their mental and physical preparations.

At this point, the golfer will sense that something is wrong. Instinct and intuition will be suggesting that all is not well. Thinking revs up. They just won't feel settled.

But the correct message is likely to be lost in the person's thinking. Or the symptoms of the thinking 'something isn't right here', will be misinterpreted.

The golfer will feel insecure, uneasy or anxious. This is simply a result of the increased flow of mental energy, not the impending golf shot, although the situation will usually be blamed as the cause.

When golfers are insecure, anxious or uneasy and don't know why, they tend not to play very well. After the round, they may well analyse what they think they were doing and come up with a reason. Usually the diagnosis will be 'a swing problem'.

It the example above, it may well feel that the downswing is coming 'over the top' of a functional plane as the arms try to get into a position where the clubface can start the ball on line.

At some point after the round, the golfer heads to the driving range to try to figure out what they were doing.

They don't pay any attention to where they aim and just start hitting balls to nowhere in particular. They might put an aim-stick or a club down to make sure they are lined up correctly, or the straight edge of the range mat gives them a subtle but effective guide as to where the target is.

In all three cases, the conflict of intentions they experienced on the golf course is no longer there, so they feel more at ease and the ball starts coming out the middle of the club.

They might feel something in their swing that they can blame for the poor round. The fix gets written down as a 'key swing thought' to be remembered next time they play.

But the same thing happens in the subsequent round. They don't align to the target correctly, and they hit some poor shots. The 'key swing thought' that wasn't really the answer anyway gets thrown out, and the whole scenario gets repeated.

Many golfers are caught in this dysfunctional feedback loop. No wonder they find it so hard to improve.

Golf Is a Mind and Body Game

When I first started to look more closely at the mental side of the game, it was mainly because I didn't have anywhere else to turn. I had a pretty good understanding of the golf swing and could hit the ball well in practice. My short game and putting were decent most of the time. So there had to be something else going on that was preventing me playing the golf I knew I was capable of.

Many golfers are similar. They can hit some good shots. This reinforces the belief that if only they played to their potential more often, they would enjoy the game far more than they do now.

But they do neither.

If you can hit the shots you want to hit on the range, the problem is not with your golf swing.

Insecure thinking leads to anxiety and tension, which disrupt the timing of the swing. You hit a bad shot when you least want to, and your swing technique gets the blame. Unfortunately, you then head off down the path of fixing the element of your game that actually works OK.

Despite what you may have been told, it is neither possible, nor necessary to build a golf swing that will hold up 'under pressure'. Golf swings don't get affected by pressure. Golfers who believe that their value, well-being and happiness depend on the outcome of a golf shot get affected by pressure.

For most coaches, the first response when a golfer is struggling is to change the golf swing. Primarily because that is where the coach's expertise lies. As instructors learn more about the mental side of the game, maybe this approach will change.

If the golfer has been playing for a while and can make solid contact with the ball on a regular basis, the problem will lie in one of two areas. The first thing I want to know is what the golfer thinks they are trying to do and why they are trying to do it.

This is where a conflict between intention and action is often revealed. Either they have poor awareness of what they are actually doing, or they have followed some external instruction and are trying to do something without really understanding the reason for doing it.

If the new movement doesn't fit with other elements of their swing or setup, the results aren't likely to be good. In both cases, there is a similar clash of intentions going on, and the golfer will sense that 'something doesn't feel right'.

This thought leads to more thinking and analysing, and the feelings of doubt that most golfers are familiar with arise.

Where 'The Yips' Originate

I have experienced 'the yips' occasionally in my own golf. Both my putting and my short game have suffered. The common belief is that the condition is a mental problem. That might be so when a case is well established, but why do they start in the first place?

My best guess is that the yips originate as a physical issue, often with setup or alignment, similar to the situation described above. The physical preparations for the shot and the intention of the swing are mismatched. Again, the golfer gets the feeling that something 'isn't right'.

This leads to thinking and analysis of what that might be. Insecure feelings, anxiety and tension in the hands and arms result. This compounds the original problem and makes the chances of a successful shot even less likely.

I had been struggling with my short game for a while. I couldn't get comfortable over the ball and had a feeling I wasn't going to strike the ball properly.

In an attempt to fix the issue, I made some adjustments to my swing. I altered my grip, tried to take the club away differently, tried a different release.

Nothing made a consistent difference.

So, I booked a lesson with Dan Grieve, head professional at Woburn Golf Club. Dan is a great coach, especially of the short game. After watching me hit a few pitches, he suggested a change to my address position. My stance and posture worked well for my full swing but were terrible for my short game.

With so much thinking about the swing itself and the outcome of the shot, I hadn't noticed that my setup was flawed. I moved my weight forward onto my left leg and tilted my spine towards the target rather than away, changing my shoulder alignment to left of the flag rather than right of it. This allowed me to strike down on the ball instead of scooping at it.

Immediately upon following Dan's suggestions, I felt I could move the club more freely and strike the ball as intended. I felt increasingly comfortable, and my thinking slowed down.

My unease and anxiety over the ball disappeared, and after a few shots, confidence returned.

Increasingly, golfers are looking to learn more about the mental side of the game. This a good thing. Understanding the relationship between thought and feeling will allow you to stay out of your own way and play your best golf more often.

But from a longer-term perspective, you might only see the benefits of this deeper understanding once the physical side of what you are doing aligns with your thinking.

You can't move a golf ball with your mind.

But the moment you stop worrying about the outcome of the shot, you are more likely to have insights that will manifest in your swing technique, short game and putting stroke. It's much easier to play your best golf when you have unity between the mental and physical sides of the game.

When the two do not match up, we feel the inconsistency of our intentions as unease, or tension.

Most golfers focus predominantly on the physical aspects of what they are doing. I suspect that's because they believe that when they can hit the ball better, the mental side of the game will take care of itself. If that's the case, why do so many tour players use mental coaches and sports psychologists?

It also might be the case that 'hard work' has become the coping strategy of choice for most golfers who want to improve. We are constantly bombarded with the message that the best golfers in the game are the hardest workers. This might appear to be the case from outside, or when someone comments on their own success in hindsight. But in the moment when they are practising, does it feel like hard work, or are they doing something they love?

In my experience, playing my best golf feels effortless. The nature of who we really are—awareness—is effortless. How can it take work to be what you already are? It only takes effort to try to be something you're not. The ego loves to think it works hard and then claims that endeavour as a badge of honour.

If you feel like you are working hard, it is a sign that you aren't seeing things clearly. That the ego is in control and is hungry for the credit.

When we play or practice with freedom and for the love of the game, the ego is nowhere to be found.

CHAPTER 9

Myth 6—Learning Golf Is Difficult

IF WE LOOK BACK THROUGH HISTORY, the presumption that human beings have an innate capacity for learning would be hard to argue against. It seems we are hardwired to adapt. To have insights and realisations that solve problems and allow us to live rich and creative lives.

We are the most evolved and broadly adapted species on the planet.

We've changed and adjusted our behaviour in response to the challenges posed by the environment long before the concept was recognised and defined as 'learning'.

We didn't need to learn how to learn.

So, is an intellectual understanding of how the learning process happens helpful, or are we just getting in our own way, making things more complicated than necessary?

In recent years, sports scientists have proposed

numerous theories around 'skill acquisition'. Learning models and concepts that try to piece together the neurological and physical processes by which talent develops. There is nothing wrong with this as such, but what are the benefits for coaches and players?

Do you know how you learned to walk, learned to talk, learned to ride your bike? Did you know at the time how you did it?

Probably not. You were a young child. You just had a go. You never questioned your ability to have new ideas, fresh insights that helped you solve problems and bring your intentions to life. You likely never wondered where they came from. Maybe trusting that it works the way it does is more important than knowing intellectually how the process happens?

Does knowing how a car works mechanically help you learn to drive it? Perhaps, but only up to a point. For example, it's useful to know that the wheels point in the direction you're steering. When you press the accelerator, the car speeds up. When you release it, it decelerates. If you want to slow down more quickly, you press the brake pedal.

Knowing the capacity of the cylinders in the engine, what the gear ratios are, or how the battery recharges is interesting information to some people. But does it really help you drive the car better?

Knowing this information might help you fix the car if it breaks down, but if the car is working, do you need it? Most people approach learning golf as if they are fixing the car, rather than learning to drive. They make it more complicated than necessary.

It is our nature to learn. We have an innate capacity to acquire new skills, to adapt our behaviour to our environment and the tools at our disposal. The potential to have insights and realisations is ever present. New thinking is always arising, allowing us to be successful in realising our intentions.

Take a moment to consider all the things you have learned to do over the years.

Using a knife and fork and writing by hand might seem mundane activities, but they require high levels of skill and dexterity. The capacity for learning is innate within all of us. We don't need to know how it works in order for it to happen. We just need to trust that it does.

Trust keeps us out of our own way. It prevents us from compromising the system and distracting ourselves with interesting but irrelevant information.

You didn't have an intellectual understanding of how to learn to run, or whistle, or balance on one leg, or clean your teeth. You identified a task, or had one suggested to you. From an awareness of the task, you formed an intention and you made an attempt.

You probably failed at first but failed better with each attempt. Eventually, it clicked.

You might have learned golf this way. Certainly, this is how the pioneers of the game would have developed. The golfers of the late 1800s proved that it is possible to become a skilful player without going to the driving range, using a launch monitor or video analysis.

Ben Hogan's Secret

In Chapter 7 of *The Three Principles of Outstanding Golf*, I suggested that we are party to an intelligence much greater than the information and knowledge we have collected in the piece of meat keeping our ears apart, if that is indeed where it is stored.

If we take our personal thinking seriously when we are learning, it seems the access to this intelligence is disrupted. When this thinking subsides, we become receptive to insight, some fresh new thinking that will move us forwards.

Everything we have ever learned has happened like this, even if we didn't see it that way at the time.

Let's look to experience to see if we can find some answers.

Can you remember a time when you were stuck at a particular point in the learning process? You worked away, grinding and struggling until frustration, fatigue or something else caused you to stop and take a break. Maybe you gave up and left what you were trying to do for another day.

As your thinking dropped away, or moved onto another concern, suddenly an idea came to you. The answer that you had been searching for in vain earlier just presented itself. Everyone I share this with has experienced something similar at a point in their lives.

One of the most famous insights in the history of the golf swing didn't happen on a golf course, on a practice fairway or at a driving range.

On April 5, 1954, *Life* magazine published an article by Ben Hogan revealing the 'secret' that he credited for his rise to the top of the game.

"I have a secret. . . It is easy to see," says Hogan, "if I tell you where to look."

According to the article, Hogan came upon his secret in September 1946, during what he considered a slump in his game. He left the Tour and went back home to Fort Worth, Texas, to work on curing the smothering hook he had battled his whole career. An idea came to him one night, and he rushed to the course at daybreak.

It worked even better than he thought it would. He started hitting his shots consistently with nice, high soft-landing fades. The hook was gone!

Hogan's secret has been discussed and argued about for the past 70 years. People are still speculating whether the secret was his weak left-hand grip, the pronation of his left wrist, the rotation of his hips in the downswing, or something else that he did not reveal.

Whatever it was, the most overlooked aspect of his insight is that it occurred at night, at his home. He didn't 'dig it out of the dirt' during one of his marathon practice sessions.

Could it be that thinking about a problem in your swing and working at it or searching for the answer might not the best way to find a solution?

Role Models of Learning

Young children are fine role models for anyone learning something new. If you watch a child learning a motor skill, you might notice a couple of things. First, there is a lot of failure going on. Second, there is little analysis or judgement. Third, there is an enormous amount of persistence and determination, but it doesn't feel like hard work.

The process works like this. There are any number of attempts that end in failure. Then a small insight or realisation occurs. Realisation happens in an instant when a fresh thought arrives. The behaviour changes.

This is how all learning occurs. We have a sudden insight that moves us forward. If we don't understand the nature of thought, we attribute our progress to the hours of practice up to that point, rather than to the change in perception.

In my experience, an insight can happen at any time. It's just more likely to happen to when thinking recedes sufficiently for the quiet voice of wisdom be heard.

We might not even realise that minor improvements are happening. More attempts are made where a different result occurs. 'Failure' may still happen, but it is different to previous failures and closer to the intention. Eventually a 'breakthrough' may occur, at which point your ego will be keen to tell the world about it, so a story is created from hindsight.

Children learn motor skills through play. They aren't deliberately trying to learn. It just happens. They may well have an idea about the task they want to complete, but they aren't attached to a particular method or even to achieving that outcome. They just go with the flow and see what evolves.

Effective, natural learning takes place without us realising. Children don't tend to have a lot of insecure thinking going on when they are playing. They aren't judging themselves. They just get on with it and their behaviour adapts to the environment.

There is some evidence to suggest that learning new motor skills becomes harder as we get older. But there is a good deal of myth and confirmation bias in that assumption.

Modern science is driven by data. Misunderstanding the nature of thought leads to misinterpretation of what is being measured. Could the experiments showing that children learn more easily than adults just be measuring the extent that adults *think* that learning is more difficult as they get older? Another self-fulfilling prophecy?

It could also be the case that adults are thinking about their learning and how they learn. Is judging and evaluating their experience all the time helping or hindering the process?

I suggest that the main reason some people find learning things later in life more difficult isn't due to physical or psychological impairment. A more likely explanation is the misunderstanding about where our feelings really come from.

If we believe that failure can make us feel insecure or incompetent, are we more or less likely to approach the learning process with enthusiasm, optimism and determination? Adults are more self-conscious (egoic) than children, and so they have a greater fear of failure.

Most golfers treat learning as an intellectual exercise. They gather more and more information, more knowledge about what they think they should be doing. Often this is an insurance policy against failing, an attempt to avoid the feelings which they think might accompany it.

By understanding the thought-feeling connection and by trusting our instincts, we judge ourselves less. There is freedom to fail. Learning becomes easier and more natural.

Knowledge Is Not the Same as Understanding

Many golfers have a lot of knowledge about what they think should be happening in their golf swing.

Unfortunately, they are less cognisant of what actually *is* happening.

Indeed, it might be said that all the knowledge they have impedes understanding of how all the different bits of information might fit together to produce a movement that sends the ball where they want it to go.

Our potential to develop skills and talent comes from the same source as our capacity to conceive activities to use them for. We have an innate capacity for learning and adaptation. It reflects the intuitive intelligence behind all scientific discoveries and works of art. These gifts combine and appear to us as creativity, wisdom and common sense.

We notice that in quieter moments, the answers to questions and the solutions to apparent problems suddenly become clear.

We become aware of the intention to do something. We have another thought about how we might make it happen. Where does this thought come from? One second, we didn't know how, next second, we did.

We might sometimes refer to it as instinctive, in that we know how to do something, but we may not really know how we know. We might not be able to explain what we are doing intellectually.

Where do our instincts to learn come from?

We didn't need to learn how to learn. If that were the case, we would need to learn how to learn how to learn.

Feel free to follow that trail of logic to a conclusion.

It's an interesting observation that when we talk about how animals learn, or how they adapt their behaviour, we are told that it is instinctive. We seem happy to leave it at that.

Yet when we are examining human behaviour, somehow the answer "it's instinctive" isn't good enough, and we feel the need to examine it and think about it further to find out how and why. We seem to have the urge not only to be able to do something well but also to be able to explain how we did it.

Expertise and intellectual concepts are valued highly by the ego and respected by other egos.

Again, this is another one of those paradoxes of the human experience. We are curious creatures, and our thirst for knowledge is one main reason we have evolved so far. Yet, at the same time, in certain areas of our lives—and learning movement seems to be one of those areas—our need to conceptualise and explain every last how and why is what trips us up.

When we acknowledge and appreciate more fully the aware space in which thought appears, we see that we always end up there when our personal thinking drops away. Understanding is the end of knowledge. All other knowledge is relative to the knowing of being.

When we respect and become more interested in the knowing by which all knowledge, insight and learning are known, insights come freely, and we come up with more good ideas. We ask different questions, which precipitate more appropriate solutions and actions than we could ever imagine were possible.

We can learn to do pretty much anything.

Unfortunately, many golfers forget that learning is innate, or have never recognised that it is so. I forgot for about 20 years. When we struggle, we immediately look outside for the solutions. There is an endless supply of information about the game. We can read books or magazines, we can go online, we can consult a golf coach or professional, we can talk to our fellow golfers.

It doesn't mean that none of these resources are helpful, but what do you think is going to be more appropriate? Allowing wisdom to come up with the best solution in this moment? Or trying to patch someone else's ideas and beliefs about what works for them onto your own body and mind?

This isn't dumbing down the debate, discounting the opinion of 'experts,' dismissing research and technology or making light of the improvements that happened in my own game after reading something or having a lesson.

But with so many opinions available to golfers, it is helpful to know you have an internal guidance system as to which pieces of information are worth listening to and maybe experimenting with, and which ones to let go.

Most of us have had the experience of trying something in our swing or putting stroke and having it feel just right from the first moment. Most of us have also had the experience of trying something that felt wrong, often at the behest of someone else, yet we persevered longer than our common sense told us we should have.

Trusting wisdom and getting curious about the nature of experience is the starting point. From here, your instincts can take you to and beyond what you thought you were capable of.

When we look back at some of the things human beings have achieved, the talents we have developed over the years, they seem miraculous. We conveniently forget that at one time we were stumbling beginners, confused and frustrated at our apparent incompetence and lack of skill.

If at that point we had listened to the thought that says, "This is too hard. Maybe this isn't the thing for you," we would never have gotten to where we are now. Instead, we followed our curiosity until insight occurred, perception changed and the difficult became easy.

In hindsight, it might look like our success was down to 'hard work' or 'perseverance'.

The ego would like that to be the case. But in the moment of learning, the ego wasn't there.

The Great Equaliser

People often talk about potential in the same context as natural talent.

We will discuss potential the final chapter of the book. A better word to describe a developing, unfulfilled talent might be *latency*. To what degree do our natural gifts determine our success? And what is the role of goal setting in maximising talent?

In a material sense, potential means making the best of whatever you've been given physically and intellectually. These are finite resources. They can be improved with training and education, but there are limits on how far they will take you. They make up a significant part of what we might think of as talent.

Whether we make the best of these attributes depends largely on whether we get in our own way. In *The Inner Game of Golf*, Tim Gallwey defines performance as 'potential minus interference'.

Every human being has the same access to the source of their experience as everyone else. What will inevitably be different for everyone is the degree to which they realise this from moment to moment. The extent to which each person feels separated from the source by their thinking is always changing.

So, if two athletes who are similar in terms of talent, technique and physical prowess are playing a match, the winner is likely to be the one who plays with freedom, clarity and presence. By staying out of their own way, they will realise more of their potential.

There are many examples in golf and other sports where the player with greater talent and physical gifts was beaten by someone who, on paper, should not have had a chance. But as the old saying goes, the game is played on grass, not on paper.

If the more-talented golfer takes their thinking seriously and gets misled by their feelings, while their opponent plays without inhibition, physical ability will be less of a factor.

Talented players often seem to have more trouble with the mental side of the game. Perhaps because they have more options for each shot and therefore more thinking to get caught up in? Talent can lead to more expectations, more layers of thought and more frustration when things take a turn for the worse.

Could 'beginner's luck'—where an inexperienced player performs way above their anticipated level—be explained by the same phenomenon, but in this case due to a lack of limiting expectations?

Success could also be down to discovering what you're good at, what you do have talent and enthusiasm for. You don't know until you try. You may be lucky and find you are good at lots of things. But a sure way to make yourself miserable is to set yourself high goals in an activity where your physical attributes don't allow you to reach the level required to achieve your ambitions.

From a wider perspective on life, singlemindedness can be more of a curse than a blessing, especially for young golfers just finding their way.

Imagine I decided now, at age 46, that my goal

was to become Olympic 100-metre champion. It doesn't matter how strong my belief is, how many intermediate goals I set, how hard I work, how good my coach is, how clear I am mentally or how much I visualise success. I simply don't have the raw sprinting speed to achieve my ambition.

If I have decided that I won't be happy unless I reach that goal, life isn't going to be much fun. The world is unlikely to change to accommodate my thoughts and feelings.

Fortunately, golf is a sport where a career can be long, and physical strength and speed are less-defining factors than in sprinting, rugby or football (although, unfortunately, this seems to be changing.) On many golf courses, a clear head and a good short game can be more-effective scoring weapons than the ability to hit the ball a huge distance.

If we believe ourselves to be a body and a mind, our talent will be limited by those perceptions. Potential lies in true nature—awareness—which has no limits. It is a power that is set free, rather than one that is applied.

Unleashing of potential allows the feats we marvel at from the world's best players to occur. We look on and remark, "I can't believe what I'm seeing here. How did they do that?"

The answer is that in the moment, the players themselves don't know how or why. They just got out of their own way and allowed their physical talents free rein.

Any of us can do this at any moment.

An important step on the path to playing the best golf you are capable of is acknowledging that you always have the capacity to learn what you need to learn. It is also normal that this capacity will often be called into doubt despite the fact that you will actually progress and improve.

Knowing this serves to inoculate you against the insecurity that every golfer feels from time to time. The game gives us every opportunity to self-sabotage, to get in our own way, to trip ourselves up.

If you take the setbacks personally, then golf will be a hard game to love, and a harder one to master. Your ego will always be telling you there is more to do, and that there is a better way of doing it. That you are not enough.

Learning is only a 'doing' in hindsight, from the perspective of the separate self. In truth, it is a by-product of understanding the true nature of experience. A recognition of unlimited potential.

Acceptance of who you really are.

CHAPTER 10

Conclusion

SO, WE HAVE COME TO the end of the book.

I hope that if golf starts to feel less enjoyable than before, at the very least, what you've read here might help you to ask some different questions.

When you do so, a different perspective can arise. Sadly, many golfers continue to ask variations of the same questions, allowing to continue unchallenged the myths and superstitions that most of the golfing world is living under.

I speak to many golfers who have a love-hate relationship with the game. The anticipation of playing is often more pleasurable than the actual experience of it. Seduced by the hope that this time will be different, they keep coming back for more.

After a few holes, the round becomes an ordeal to be battled through. A trial to be endured and overcome in order to reach a predetermined outcome, rather than an experience to be savoured and enjoyed.

They walk off the 18th green relieved if they have met their expectations, disappointed and discouraged if they haven't. How many reviews of the round at the 19th hole start with

"If only . . . ?"

Our motivation for playing often comes from a desire to challenge ourselves, to prove something. Could finding the balance between challenge and achievement be the key to a more enjoyable, more fulfilling relationship with the game?

Only if we believe that the game of golf has the power to make us feel the way we feel. I hope you are starting to see that this is cannot be the case. Who or what is trying to prove something to whom?

Improvements in equipment and agronomy over the past 30 years have made it easier than ever before to take up the game and become reasonably competent. Are recreational golfers playing better and enjoying the game more than they did 30 years ago? Diminishing numbers of golfers in established playing nations around the world would suggest not.

The relationship many people have with their

golf is mirrored in the rest of their lives. An ongoing search for objects, achievements and relationships in which they hope they will find happiness. Or the resistance of circumstances that might deprive them of the feeling.

Many of us allowed our experience of the game of golf to be tainted by this underlying misunderstanding about life. The real problems lie not with the game, but with us. Or, more accurately, with who we think we are?

Persistent feelings of mild dissatisfaction, of wanting, seem to be the default setting, the status quo, the day-to-day norm for many people. Our culture tells us the remedy for these feelings is action, attainment, success.

We get glimpses of contentment or joy when we hit a good drive off the first tee, or when we play the front nine below our handicap. The neediness ends for a short while. But this satisfaction and contentment are fleeting.

Almost immediately we worry anew about when and how it will go wrong. About what we need to do to maintain our form and our state of mind. It's back to the search for answers and solutions. Back to the struggle.

Hopefully, this isn't you. Hopefully, curiosity was your motive for picking up this book rather than frustration. Hopefully, it has prompted some different questions as to why you feel the way you do about your golf.

The question asked in Chapter 2 was "Why are you reading this book?" That seems simple enough, but it's actually a different question in disguise.

"What game are you playing?"

Clues will be found in the way you feel and the way you behave on the course. Are you feeling frustrated, anxious and insecure? When those feelings arise, do you fight them, do you try to control or avoid them, or are you learning from them?

If you get tense and nervous on the first tee or feel angry when your play doesn't match your expectations, you berate yourself after bad shots, chances are you have stopped playing golf in favour of a different game.

The game of golf involves hitting a ball into a hole with a stick. There is no purpose or meaning to the pursuit, other than that thoughts have attached to it. The feelings around the game of golf have everything to do with our level of understanding. Nothing to do with the activity itself.

The game is always neutral.

The human experience is relative. One of separation, of objects and things. This view of the world is purely conceptual, a figment of the mind.

It is a foundational misunderstanding expressed in a dysfunctional relationship between a limited concept of who we really are and an invented meaning we have attached to the game.

Our ever-shifting responses to this misunderstanding determine how we feel before, during and after we play. Experience is real, what we think we are experiencing is not.

A golfer who is struggling typically suffers from identification with this illusion They have forgotten who they really are and have stopped playing golf, turning it instead into another game in an effort to feel better. The ego has decided that golf is the medium by which it will fortify itself. To become something, or someone more than it believes itself to be.

In the Introduction, I asked the question, "Can a human being control or divert the flow of thought?"

The answer is no, because from the perspective of the true self—awareness—a human being *is* a thought. A perception, a story about who we think we are.

The remedy for a lack of enjoyment is not a change of golf swing, a change of coach, a change of equipment or a change of scenery. When suffering golfer takes a break from the game, what they are actually taking a break from is the pressure of living up to their story, their ego-driven expectations. A break from them 'self'.

The struggle can only end with the realisation that they are not the limited, finite body-mind that they appear to be.

Realising Your Potential

A significant moment in the career of any golfer, regardless of level of play, is the moment they 'realise their potential.'

As touched on in the previous chapter, from the materialist paradigm—the perspective of time and space—this would be defined as making the most of your latent abilities, proven by achieving some sort of external milestone. Perhaps getting down to a single-figure handicap, breaking par for the first time, winning a monthly medal, gaining a tour card, winning a first tournament or perhaps a Major Championship.

There is a different perspective.

To me, the point where you realise your potential is when you see true nature. That there is one fundamental reality—consciousness. The word 'potential' comes from the Latin *potent*, which means 'being able'; and *potentia*, which means 'power'.

It's a powerful moment when you realise who or what you really are. This enlightenment is what all experience is pointing towards.

It's when you come home to the deeper understanding that 'you' and your experience are in fact two sides of the same coin. That there is unity behind the diversity.

There have been moments on the golf course when you have experienced the freedom, happiness, love, peace and fulfilment that comes with knowing true nature. When you hit that perfect shot and all wanting, seeking and resisting ends for a few moments. If that had never been the case, why would you continue to seek those feelings through the game?

In moments of your best play, you've been guided by a deep, spiritual intelligence. You allowed an awesome creative power to manifest, resulting in golf shots of which you didn't realise you were capable.

Afterwards, you might have had the sense that you were the awareness of the thoughts about what was happening. The witness rather than the servant of those thoughts.

In such moments, infinite potential was realised through you. In hindsight, you see that what you had assumed you were capable of, what you believed would make you happy, what you'd thought was the purpose of your life, had been restrained only by the limitations of your own mind.

You saw beyond your intellectual knowledge to infinite resources, accessible at any moment.

When you are playing your best golf, or performing anything well, you don't really know how you are doing what you are doing. Action just flows. Decisions are made instinctively without contemplation. When the moment has passed, you might not be able to recall what happened.

Any explanation is added retrospectively. You may have felt that you were in a high state of awareness in the moment, but there wasn't an intensity or a striving. You might have had a similar experience when you came to the end of a car journey but couldn't remember large chunks of it.

This is because 'you' weren't really controlling or creating the activity. The energy and intelligence that generated the performance was not a product of the ego. It became a reality arising *at the same time as and from the same source as* the separate self, what you think of as 'you'.

Afterwards, if there is credit to be claimed, the ego will be first in the queue.

As described in Chapter 6, the separate self is not really an entity. The description of it as such is a concession to the limitations of language. It is an activity of awareness, as is the performance it claims as its own. The actor is not separate from the play. They are part of the same whole.

When this is understood, when there is trust, the ego can relax. It can stop being driven by feelings of neediness or lack. There is no separation. It goes 'home'.

It is replaced with a sense of 'knowing' that whatever happens, well-being cannot be damaged or improved by failure or success in the world of form.

Life unfolds, rather than feeling like a struggle and a grind. Trying to force success with willpower, with strategies or techniques no longer makes sense. You are free.

Pause for a moment to reflect on all the success and achievement you've had in life. Don't take anything for granted.

Learning to walk, learning to talk, driving a car,

using a knife and fork, using a computer, reading a book, building and maintaining relationships. All are highly sophisticated activities that have been learned and mastered.

Your ego will whisper that you worked hard for your achievements, and that the struggle was what made you who you are, what separates you from the masses, from those unwilling or unable.

But did it feel like that in the moment? Or was that a story made up after the fact by a fictional entity keen to burnish its own sense of importance?

You probably think differently about these everyday skills than you do about your golf? Maybe you believe that being a good golfer takes more talent, more skill, more innate ability than it does to do these things?

I can assure you it does not.

The main obstacle to you reaching the same level of effortless competence in your golf as you have in other areas of life is simply that you have some thinking about your golf that you don't have elsewhere. This thinking veils awareness. It impairs trust in intuition and blocks potential, so it seems harder to experience the same freedom and clarity on the golf course than it does off it.

Success seems further away the harder you try.

At any moment, you can relax and trust that you have what you need to learn what you need to learn. Trust that you have what you need to play well when you want to play well. When you realise that you can perform and enjoy the game without working hard and grinding away, you are home.

You have realised your potential.

Why Do You Play Golf?

Let's return to the question posed at the start of Chapter 2 and covered in more depth at the start of Chapter 4. We are often told that we need to know our 'Why?'. According to the standard way of thinking, if we know why we play, then our belief, motivation and desire will flow from this overriding clarity of purpose. Knowing why we play seems important.

But is this true?

Let's look at what this 'Why?' really is.

At the basic level of experience, 'Why?' is a thought. Although it doesn't appear that way, all thoughts are created equal. They are just manifestations of spiritual energy revealing itself as memories, imaginings, perceptions or sensations. They arise in awareness and then disappear.

So why do we persist with treating some

thoughts with more seriousness than others?

Most people have a kind of thought hierarchy in their minds. Beliefs are most important. The thoughts that guide most people's lives. They often come with a supporting network of thoughts and concepts to back them up. These thoughts are mainly memories. The reason why you play golf probably falls into this category.

You played golf in the past, and you felt happy. 'Happiness comes from golf' became your belief. Beliefs are sticky. They hang around.

There are other ideas and theories floating around in the middle ground. These include practical thoughts that are useful in conducting business or daily life. Once they have been considered and any actions taken, they disappear. Then there is a barely noticed random flow of perceptions, memories and imaginations near the bottom.

All of them are made of the same stuff, and one is no more serious than another, other than in the relative importance we give them. A judgement comprising more thought. The framework of supporting thoughts we build around a belief held dear to us is perhaps why we take it more seriously than other thoughts.

The 'Why?' thought looks important because it appears that reasoning—and therefore, consequences—will flow from resolving it. For many people, the 'Why?' is the foundation stone that holds the whole edifice of a belief together.

But again, is that true?

At the most fundamental level, when we have peeled back the layers of thinking that veil our direct experience, the 'Why?' question is the one that has no answer.

Or, it has one answer that might not be an answer at all.

The answer to "Why?" is simply "Because".

The question is one that seekers, philosophers, leaders have been asking since the beginning of time. Yet the 'Why?' question is a product of the intellect, not of true nature.

Who we really are doesn't need to know why. It doesn't even understand the question. For there to be a why, there would need to be a cause and an effect: two things, separation, duality.

If there is only consciousness, one reality, the question does not exist. The overwhelming evidence from our direct experience, when thinking is stripped away, is that this is true.

When a child first starts to play a game, there is no 'Why?'. It just is what it is. Play is an expression of happiness. A form of creativity, in the same way that art, music or dance are expressions of creativity.

We play because we can. We don't need a reason to create. It's part of what we fundamentally are.

To prescribe a reason reduces it to the functionality of work, of duress, of need.

Play is noble, light-hearted. It springs from freedom. It is born of inspiration rather than from obligation. It points to true nature.

To suggest there is an answer to the question 'Why?' implies necessity. Who we really are does not lack and therefore has no need.

When we start to ask 'Why?', it's because we have turned play into work. In work, we are trying to become someone we are not. In play, we remember who we really are.

Are You Getting in Your Own Way?

Many golfers, in quiet moments of reflection, are aware of what seem a set of limiting beliefs 'holding them back'. The traditional sports psychology approach would be to examine each of these beliefs one by one. To try to unpick the web of supporting thoughts and beliefs until the belief dies and behaviour changes.

This approach can be successful. But it's a bit like picking up individual leaves from the lawn in the autumn. You think you've finished the job, then a gust of wind comes along and you're back where you started.

What I'm suggesting is different. I'm suggesting we cut down the tree. Look beyond all the beliefs you have—or could have—about yourself, and to look towards what is aware of those beliefs.

From where do they arise? Who or what believes them? What is aware of all that thinking about who you are and what you can and cannot do? Could that be who you really, truly are?

Your true self is not who you think you are and what you think you are capable of. All of that is your ego. The ego is made of thought, of thinking. And as we know, thinking can and does change from moment to moment. Hence, confidence in our abilities comes and goes.

What comes and goes—what changes—cannot be the truth. Truth is always true. It doesn't come or go. Who you really are is awareness of the story you are telling yourself about who you think you are. The entity referred to with the words "I am".

What if the thing stopping you from experiencing happiness and fulfilment is the thinking you have? The thinking that says in order to achieve it, you need to be something different, something more than you already are.

Intellectually, this might make sense. Thought says, "If you were already good enough, then you'd be where you wanted to be?"

Right?

Unfortunately, not.

It's a vicious circle. A catch-22 situation. A paradox. If you think about it, the recurring story you have been telling yourself your whole golfing life is one of becoming. That you need to become better, you need to change, to improve in order to be happy. In order to feel free, to feel confident.

How is that working out for you? Maybe that approach has taken you as far as it can.

Perhaps it's time for that story to stop. Maybe it's worth trying to just relax into your potential and stop fighting, stop struggling. See how it feels to accept the possibility that maybe you already have got what you need, or that when you need it, you'll find a way without a plan, a strategy or a technique.

What I hope you will take from this book is the solid understanding that you already are what you are trying to become. Always have been, always will be.

If that's the case, golf becomes an expression of happiness. There is nothing to lose and nothing to gain.

Just because you have some thinking going on and don't feel great at this moment, those thoughts and that feeling have no power to affect the way you swing the golf club.

The more you trust this, believe it and respect it, the better you will play and the more enjoyable your golf will be. Sometimes, people will ask me, "How can I trust and believe that I have this potential when I see all this evidence pointing me in the opposite direction?"

Remember that you are viewing the 'evidence' through the window of your current beliefs, your thoughts, fears and limitations.

If you don't really understand the nature of the window—your limited, finite mind—how can you understand whether the view you are seeing is accurate?

Often, taking the first step can seem like the hardest one of all.

The good news is that all you have to do for that first step is open up to the possibility that golf—and life—might work differently from how we were told. As soon as that happens, expectations drop away, and you can settle down.

You then have a chance to hear what wisdom, intuition might be whispering to you.

Most people who are struggling with their golf are familiar with doubt. But you can't have doubt unless you believe that certainty exists.

Perhaps the next step on the path to your best, most consistent, most enjoyable golf, should simply be to doubt your doubt.

"Happiness is simply the knowing of our own being
– its knowing of itself – as it is.
To abide knowingly, as that is pure meditation and,
In the end, turns out to be life itself.
Happiness is the highest spiritual practice."

Rupert Spira

Dear Reader,

Well, here we are. I guess you could think of this page as the 19th Hole.

As with a game of golf, this could go one of two ways.

If you didn't enjoy the book, you will probably just want to neck your lime and soda and get the hell out of here. I'm sorry if your experience didn't match your expectations.

Perhaps you will give it another go one day? After all, our thoughts and feelings change all the time.

If you enjoyed the book, we could hang out for a while. Savour a few beers, recall the good bits, think about how the bad bits could be better and look forward to the next time.

I'm happy to buy the first round. By way of reciprocation, it would be lovely if you could leave a short review with the retail outlet from which you purchased?

If you fancy another round sometimes soon, you might well enjoy my other book, The Three Principles of Outstanding Golf.

You can find it on Amazon UK.

If you'd like to get in touch to have chat about your golf, or if you'd like to learn more about the ideas you have read in the book, please drop me an email to sam@samjarmangolf.com.

You can find my website at samjarmangolf.com, find me on Twitter @samjarmangolf, or on Facebook at facebook.com/samjarmangolf.

Thanks again for reading, and all the best with your golf.

Kind regards,
Sam

About the author

Sam Jarman is a professional golfer, coach, author and speaker.

He played full time tournament golf for ten years, before he realised that helping other golfers to stop make the same mistakes he was making could be more enjoyable and more lucrative than continuing to make them himself.

His first book *The Three Principles of Outstanding Golf*, is a 50,000 word summary of the most significant thing he has learned; keep it simple.

"I finally saw the reason I was struggling to be the golfer I wanted to be. I also saw that the misunderstanding which prevents golfers from performing to their potential, is also responsible for the stress, worry, anxiety, boredom and lack of fulfilment which many people endure in their day to day lives.

I much prefer it when the people I know and like are enjoying what they do, so when I'm not playing tournaments, I help golfers and other athletes play better, learn better, work better and live better.

When we see our true nature, it frees us to be more inspired and productive, to enjoy life and work rather than endure them, and to be ourselves more often."

Sam lives near Woburn Golf Club in Buckinghamshire with Daisy, a pretty but slightly unreliable cocker spaniel. When he isn't teaching, writing or playing golf he spends his time salmon fishing, skiing, reading, poker and enjoying the occasional pint of Guinness.